Guided

BY GRACE

Laura K. Meier, Esq.

450 Newport Center Drive, Suite 500
Newport Beach, California 92660

www.guidedbygraceplanning.com

imprimatur granted February 8, 2024 by Most Reverend Kevin William Vann, J.C.D.,D.D.

Nihil obstat - Rev. William B. Goldin, S.Th.D.
The Nihil obstat is a declaration that a book or pamphlet is considered to be free
from doctrinal or moral error. It is not implied that those who have granted the Nihil
obstat agree with the contents, opinions or statements expressed.

Printed in the United States of America.

ISBN: 978-1-63385-502-1

Published by
Word Association Publishers
205 Fifth Avenue
Tarentum, Pennsylvania 15084

www.wordassociation.com
1.800.827.7903

Guided
BY GRACE

A CATHOLIC JOURNEY *THROUGH*
WILLS, TRUSTS, AND ESTATE PLANNING

LAURA K. MEIER, ESQ.

CONTENTS

INTRODUCTION

Have you ever been in a situation that felt so out of your control that all you could do was pray and plead with God to intervene? When my youngest son, Andrew, was three years old, he and several other children were out playing on a greenbelt behind our home. I went inside for a moment to order pizza for them, but when I came back out, I didn't see him. I called for him, but he didn't come out from behind the bushes or trees like I thought he would. I began asking the other kids where he had gone but no one seemed to know. I went back inside the house, thinking I must have missed him coming in, but he wasn't there either. I began to worry.

I checked the greenbelt again, and the connecting one, and the next, but he was nowhere to be found. Neighbors began coming out of their homes to help me find him upon hearing the panic in my voice. Soon, my husband and friends rushed over, and even the police came to help.

I recall the exact moment when I felt completely and utterly helpless. It had been forty minutes since I'd last seen

Andrew. I had looked everywhere from the distant cliff to the streets, to the gutters, to the bushes, under beds, trunks of cars—anywhere he could possibly be. Andrew was gone and no one could seem to find him anywhere, including me, his own mother. Completely powerless, I hung my head in that moment and plead with God to intervene.

We were so fortunate that day. The police soon found Andrew walking with a good Samaritan who was trying to help him find his way home. Andrew was back in our arms safe and sound, and our nightmare was finally over. Thanks be to God.

We all experience helpless moments like this in life when all we can seem to do is hang our head and plead with God to save us, or help us, or comfort us. As an estate planning lawyer who helps people navigate life's most difficult moments like a medical crisis or death, I see first-hand how overwhelming and chaotic those situations can be, and how quickly life can change. And while professionals like me can help families navigate those difficult situations just like those first responders helped me find Andrew, it is ultimately the presence of God that we long for most during our greatest times of need.

Yet many of us, who take the time to create a plan to protect ourselves and loved ones during a medical crisis or death, tend to consider only the legal and practical considerations, like who should oversee our affairs or at what age our children should receive their inheritance. We treat our planning for end-of-life matters as a secular transaction where we can "check the box" and move on, hoping that all will play out well. We don't ask questions like, how does God intend for my assets to be passed on, or what type of care does He long for me to receive if I am seriously hurt or ill? This oversight leaves us with a half protective plan that doesn't fully reflect our true wishes.

And that's if we even take time to create a plan at all. Most families do not.

Most families don't address these inevitable difficult life situations until they are forced to like when they receive an alarming medical report or are told that a loved one has died. Once families are in crisis mode, everything becomes turmoil. Minor children can end up in the care of strangers because the parents didn't name guardians for them. The family can end up in a long and expensive court process known as probate that can take years to resolve. Money can end up unnecessarily going to the government or get taken by ill-intentioned third parties, instead of going to the intended beneficiaries. Medical decisions can't be made by the family and information is withheld from them. And suddenly the loved one who has died is remembered as a wonderful person who unfortunately left their loved ones with a mess on their hands.

Many families end up fighting and, in some cases, become completely torn apart.

I know you wouldn't want this outcome for your family, and I don't either, but it is unfortunately the reality for far too many families who fail to meaningfully plan.

What if there was a better way? What if there was a way that, if you were to become sick or pass away, your family could make decisions on your behalf in unison with the complete care and protections that Jesus longs for you to have? That no one would be hauled into a courtroom to sort out your affairs and your family would be spared from chaos and contention? That your money would be immediately available to those who depend on you and used for good, and be safe-guarded from predators, creditors, divorce, and lawsuits? That your minor children would be raised by who you want and in a home that honors God's dream for their upbringing? And what if you could be remembered as someone who lived their life for God, and benefited your family, the church, and the community, even in your final act?

And, what if at the core of your plan for these end-of-life matters were the protections and grace that Jesus offers all of us in our greatest times of need?

Now, I am not suggesting you must have some sort of pre-plan in place if you want God to show up in your most difficult moments. I can assure you He will be there regardless. But friends, we are indeed blessed that our Catholic Faith offers us a great richness of guidance to draw from when planning for these difficult life matters. From ensuring our children would continue to be raised in the faith, to receiving the Sacraments of the Anointing of the Sick and Viaticum, to leaving behind a legacy that can bless the generations to come, we can create a plan for our family that is both practical and holy.

During our time together in this book, I will show you the legal and practical steps you can take to protect yourself and your loved ones during a medical crisis or death. But I am going to take it a step further and explore alongside you the different ways we can also include God's best for us into our decision-making, based on teachings from the Holy Bible, the Catechism of the Catholic Church, and the United States Conference of Catholic Bishops. As a dear friend put it, you will be getting both the *plain*-glass and the *stained*-glass version of creating a plan for your family. No matter whether you consider yourself a *good* Catholic or a *good enough* Catholic or call another place of worship home, I invite you to take this universal faith-based guidance to heart.

And you might just find, like I did, a new appreciation for the thoroughness of the Catholic Faith perspective, the love that God has for all His children in this world, and a desire to change how we live today as we think about what we hope to leave behind for tomorrow…

"Do not let your hearts be troubled, you have faith in God," Jesus assures us[1]. How wonderful it is knowing that we have a God who loves us and has promised every one of His children, no matter who they are or what they have or have not done, that He loves us and will never forsake us in our time of need. We should take comfort in knowing He will be there for us no matter what. "Even though I walk through

---

1   John 14:1

the valley of the shadow of death, I will fear no evil, for you are with me; your rod and your staff comfort me."[2]

Friend, God loves you so deeply and longs to be present in your life, in your suffering, and in your transition into eternal life. Let's look together now at how you can best create a faith-based plan that protects you and your loved ones, and pre-invites Jesus to be there with you each step of the way.

2   Psalms 23:4

Chapter 1

THE **DEFAULT PLAN**

If you are like most people, you don't yet have a plan in place that addresses what should happen if you get seriously ill or pass away. In the legal world, we call this type of plan an *estate plan*. Most people refer to the estate planning process as "making a will".

I help families create estate plans through my private law practice in California and often educate families on this topic through my community workshops, my books, or in the media. I always pose this question to families, and I'll ask you this question now too:

What percentage of adults do you think already have an estate plan?

I usually hear guesses like—5%, 20%, 10%, and so on. No one guesses too high which I think is because subconsciously they are hoping they aren't the only family who has put this off! And, then there's always at least someone who comes in with 1% because they have no faith that any of us have gotten our affairs in order! What was your guess?

You might be surprised, like others, when I tell you that **100% of adults already have an estate plan, including *you*.**

Confused? Well, that's because if you have not yet created your own estate plan for your family, your state will step in with their own default estate plan, and as a spoiler alert, you're not going to like it!

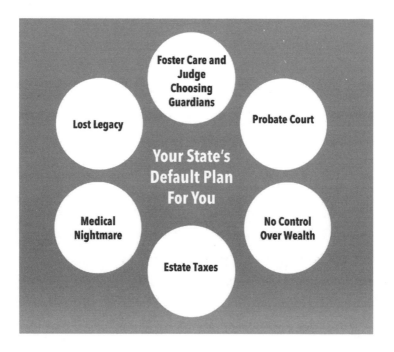

This default chart shows all the areas of your life that will have to be dealt with if you face a medical crisis or pass away. Your state's plan will subject your family to years of courtrooms and lawyers and determine everything from who should raise your kids, to who should control your money, and even whether you can be kept on artificial life support if you're in a vegetative state.

While there are a lot of things the state will have to do for you that you won't like, there are also a lot of things they *won't* do for you—which is even worse—such as ensuring the money you left behind is immediately available to your loved ones and safeguarded from ill-intentioned third parties; to preventing funds from unnecessarily going to the government and taxes, to preserving your personal legacy. And never mind that your state will NOT incorporate any of your religious preferences or practices at all in their default plan for your family!

If you want to know if the state's plan is a good one for you or not, just ask someone who has lost a loved one and had to turn to the state to clean up their affairs. They would do anything to go back in time and have their loved one create an estate plan. It truly is a nightmare and knowing it could have been completely avoided makes it all the worse.

The good news is that you can avoid your state's default plan by setting up your own estate plan that is fully designed to meet the needs of your unique family. By incorporating the legal, practical, and spiritual protections you need, your family can have a complete plan and most of all, peace of mind. Let's go through the state's default plan now and learn about how to best avoid it. Imagine how good it will feel knowing your options!

Chapter 2

THE **PHYSICAL CARE** OF YOUR CHILDREN

If you are the parent of a minor child, you will want to pay close attention to what I am going to share with you about their care (or lack of) if you prematurely pass away.

Even if your kids are grown and you are so glad you no longer worry about this, I am here to tell you that if your adult children do not make plans for this scenario, by default the courts will drag you and the other set of grandparents into a long and painful guardianship proceeding that can unnecessarily pit families against one another. So, I encourage you to get educated on this issue rather than skip ahead, and better understand how you can support whoever serves in the guardianship role.

Our love for our kids (and grandkids) is unconditional and everlasting. Sure, they drive us crazy now and then, and young parents miss their sleep and free time, but there's nothing in the world any of us would trade for having these kids in our lives. The Holy Bible says that "Children are a gift from the Lord; they are a reward from him" and that "grand-children are the crown of the aged."[3]

Even greater is the love that God has for our children. Recall the story in the Holy Bible about how Christ rebuked his disciples for trying to turn the children away when their parents sought a blessing for them. Stopping his exchange with the Pharisees, Christ said, "Let the children come to me, and do not prevent them; for the kingdom of heaven belongs to such as these."[4] Christ demonstrated to us in this encounter what a priority His children are to him.

I know as a parent of four growing kids how difficult it is to even imagine something happening to us that would prevent us from raising our kids. But, as we are aware, we are mortal. We are reminded of this every time we turn on the news or hear about a friend of a friend. You may even have personal experience with losing a loved one.

Unfortunately, if the unexpected does happen to a parent, and there is not a plan in place for the children's care, the state must step in with its own default plan which often involves temporary foster care, courtrooms, heartbreak, and turmoil.

---

3   Psalms 127:3; Proverbs 17:6

4   Matthew 19:14

STATE LAW

> If parents become incapacitated or die, their minor children can be placed in temporary foster care, and a judge will have to decide who should raise them, unless the parents have legally named temporary and permanent legal guardians for them.

There was a family in San Diego, California several years ago where the husband and wife were tragically killed in a car accident, leaving behind three young children. Rather than the children immediately going into the care of extended family members, the children were instead temporarily placed in the care of strangers, and for over a year the aunts battled in court over who should be the guardians. The Judge ultimately placed them in the care of one of the aunts, into a family that was now completely torn apart.

This heartbreaking story is the last thing any of us would want for our children, but it is unfortunately what happens when parents fail to make legal plans for who should raise their kids. To prevent a tragedy like this from happening in your own family, it's critical that you establish both a long-term care plan and a short-term care plan for raising your children should something unexpected happen to you.

Creating a Long-Term Care Plan for Raising Your Kids

If something were to happen to either you or your spouse, someone else would have to step in and raise your children. In the legal world, we call this person a permanent guardian. If you do not legally identify a permanent guardian in advance, then a judge who doesn't even know you or your family would have to step in and choose one, which can take a year or more in court and pit family members against one another.

Choosing a guardian can be a tough decision. I've heard so many times from parents that they put off setting up their estate plan because they and their spouse can't agree on who the guardian for their children should be. Even my husband and I have struggled with this, and we are supposed to be the experts! If it's tough for us parents to decide, imagine how much harder it is for a judge who has never even met our family. It is our moral and legal responsibility as parents to make this decision and not delay. The good news is I have a process that can help you with that!

Easy Three-Step Process for Choosing Permanent Guardians

Our easy three step process can help you better identify who would make a great potential guardian based on what matters most to the parents when it comes to raising kids. While this easy three step process isn't magic, it usually helps provide parents more clarity on what matters most. We are fortunate that our Catholic faith can help guide us in this decision.

As I share the legal, practical, and spiritual considerations with you both, please try and give yourself (and your spouse) some grace before prematurely vetoing suggestions. We don't want any husbands on the couch tonight or anyone having to backtrack or apologize![5]

Step One

Take out a blank piece of paper and write down all the people who love your children and could potentially serve as guardians. Parents typically consider people like grandparents, aunts and uncles, cousins, adult siblings, godparents, friends, coworkers, or in my case, anyone who would be willing to finish raising four kids! Ideally, you will write down at least five to seven names. Again, try to resist evaluating these people or shooting down names until you complete all three steps.

Now, a note about godparents in case they're on your list. A common myth is that godparents are legally and morally obligated to raise their godchildren if something happens to the parents. This is false. Instead, the Code of Canon law only requires godparents to "help the baptized lead a Chris-

---

5   The three step process is based on a process created by our colleague Ali Katz, Esq., Founder of Personal Family Lawyer.

tian life in keeping with baptism and to fulfill faithfully the obligations inherent in it." Thus, a godparent's obligation is for their godchild's spiritual formation, not for their physical care. You may still wish to include them, however, on your list of potential guardians.

Step Two

Put away your list of those potential people you identified for a moment and don't think about who you wrote down. Clear your mind, and now take out a separate blank piece of paper. It's time to really think about your priorities when it comes to raising your kids—priorities you expect a potential guardian to honor.

Most parents consider priorities like keeping the kids in the family, not making the kids move away, making sure the guardians will be young or healthy enough to finish raising the kids, having a married couple so there are two hands on deck, or that the guardians have the same education level or religious beliefs as the parents. All of these are great and practical priorities to consider. (One thing we do not want parents to consider, however, is the potential guardian's financial resources. It is our responsibility as parents to leave enough money behind for our children's care. This is typically accomplished through life insurance until the family has enough resources that cover all child-rearing costs.)

As you contemplate what priorities matter most for your children's upbringing, we should not only consider the practical considerations, but the spiritual considerations as well.

One of the most powerful resources we have as Catholics, in addition to the Holy Bible, is the Catechism of the Catholic Church. Based on teachings from the Holy Bible, the Mass, the Sacraments, Catholic teachings and tradition, and the lives of the saints, the Catechism offers us extensive guidance to draw from when making consequential decisions like this. You might be surprised like I was as an adult convert to Catholicism, that the Catechism is not a book of black and white rules, but rather a beautiful vision of God's dream for our lives. This vision includes the type of home He wants our children—*His children*—to be raised in, including what priorities matter most to Him.

Catholic teachings provide that God's first priority for our children's upbringing and care is a **loving home**. God longs for His children to be raised in homes where they are "regarded as children of God and respected as human persons."[6] We as parents (or guardians) should "create a home where tenderness, forgiveness, respect, fidelity, and disinterested service are the rule," and where our children are "spiritually and physically provided for."[7] Our children belong in a home environment where they are well-loved and cared for and treated with respect as children of God.

---

6   Catechism 2226-2228
7   Catechism 2226-2228

Next, God's second priority for our children's upbringing is their **spiritual education**. God calls us parents (and guardians) to "educate our children to fulfill God's laws" and "educate them in virtues." This is because "a wholesome family life can foster interior dispositions that are a genuine preparation for a living faith and remain a support for it throughout one's life."[8] God calls us to lay a strong spiritual foundation for our children so they know they can turn to him throughout their lives, and not have to navigate this world without him.

How many children are not being taught inside their homes that they were created by a Father in Heaven who loves them? Or sadly, that God is some distant figure who is always pointing his finger at them in disappointment? How many children experience this broken world mistakenly believing that they are alone, and nothing bigger exists for them? No wonder our children's generation is experiencing an alarming mental health crisis. That was not God's dream for His children. God says we parents must educate our children in such a manner that they can form a direct relationship with Him and go through life experiencing His unfailing love and support.

Finally, God's third priority for our children is **protection**. God wants His children to be raised in a home that is "protected from the decay of the world." Parents and guardians are to "teach our children to subordinate the material

---

8   Catechism 2225

and instinctual dimensions to interior and spiritual ones" and "avoid the compromising and degrading influences which threaten human societies."[9] Instead, parents and guardians should "evangelize their children...teach their children to pray...and discover their vocation as children of God."

In an era where so many dark forces are telling our children they're not good enough, or weren't made right, or won't get the right opportunities in life because they have the wrong genetics or zip code, our homes should be a fortress for them where they can learn the truth: That they were "wonderfully made"[10] and that God has promised, "I know well the plans I have in mind for you, plans for your welfare and not for woe, so as to give you a future hope."[11]

I don't know about you but understanding more about God's dream for our children's upbringing made me really stop and think, not just about my priorities for choosing a potential guardian, but more so about the type of home my husband and I are providing today for our children. Anyone else's home need less YouTube and more encouragement and prayer? I know how easy it is for us parents to get caught up in the world's priorities for our kids like a great zip code or the right schools. And while yes, those considerations are important, God is saying it's not really about where your home is located or whether your kids are Harvard bound; It's more

---

9   Catechism 2224

10   Psalms 139:14

11   Jeremiah 29:11

about what goes on *inside* our homes and what our children are being taught about Him that matters most.

Step Three

Compare the first sheet that lists your potential guardians with the second sheet that lists your top three priorities. Now, rank in order the "potential people" you listed, from first choice down to last choice, based on who offers or possesses most, if not all, of your top three priorities when it comes to raising kids. That should give you a nice list to work off when identifying who would make a great choice for guardianship. Be sure to legally designate your first choice, second choice, and third choice in case someone cannot serve if the time comes.

Now, some parents will find that the people on their list aren't able to offer the top three priorities they identified when it comes to raising their kids. I know that's tough, especially when you want to honor God and give your family the best, but that's where the rest of us as part of your Catholic community come in.

Catholic teachings provide that we are all part of a single "Christian Family" that is "a community of faith, hope, and charity."[12] The Christian family "has a duty to live in such a way that its members learn to care and take responsibility for the young, the old, the sick, the handicapped, and the poor".[13]

---

12   Catechism 2204

13   Catechism 2208

The Catholic Church understands that "there are many families who are at times incapable of providing help for the young… and it devolves on other persons, other families, and in a subsidiary way, society, to provide for their needs."[14] The Holy Bible says that "Religion that is pure and undefiled before God and the Father is this: to care for orphans and widows in their affliction."[15]

So how can we help best support other families who may need that extra support from the Christian community, especially if a parent has passed away?

I recall what happened a few years ago with a family I know when the mother was diagnosed with breast cancer while the children were still young. Her extended family, her local community, and her church community (The Church of Jesus Christ of Latter-Day Saints) all rallied around her to provide her and her husband and children a lot of care and support. Eventually, this young mother "returned to her Heavenly Father" as her family shared when they announced her passing. As you can imagine, even with great faith, this was an incredibly difficult outcome for the family and all who loved her.

While her husband has done a remarkable job continuing to care for their son and daughter and raise them in their faith, their grandmother recently shared with me how their church family has also continued to rally around this family

---

14   Catechism 2208

15   James 1:27

and offer support for their everyday needs. From help with running errands, social outings, religious formation, and emotional support, their church family has been there each step of the way. There's also a group of men from the church who continue to take the father out for a bike ride and pizza each week and give him a safe place to talk and feel support.

Is this not the exact manifestation of what Christ means when he calls us as a Christian Family to care for orphans and widows in their affliction?

As you evaluate your final choices for permanent guardians, make sure you also include a list of those from your Christian Family that your guardians can count on for support and for assistance with the children's continued faith formation and inclusion. And let's also think about how we can better forge those relationships today, so our children will always have a strong support system. Take time to look left, and look right, when you're grabbing that donut after Mass and introduce yourself to another family or join a small faith group or ministry. The Christian Family is counting on you and me to help with our children's upbringing, especially during a crisis.

Documenting Your Long-Term Care Plan

Your wishes for guardianship must be legally formalized. Telling a friend who you want, or sending a text to your mom when your flight is about to take off is not sufficient. Most states require that guardianship designation be formalized through a Will. In some states, it can also be documented in a stand-alone form, commonly referred to as a Nomination of Permanent Guardian Form. Like all legal formalities, you will want to consult with your estate planning lawyer on what your state requires.

You will also want to document what other important people you want to participate in your children's upbringing. We use what is called an Instructions of Guardians form to identify these people and lay out the parents' vision for their children's upbringing. It's especially important to document your wishes for grandparent visitation as many states will grant visitation to grandparents if the surviving parent or guardian does not adequately facilitate this. Hopefully, this is not the case for any of our family situations but it's still important to consider, especially in cases of divorce.

As we conclude this chapter on our children's care, let me encourage you to formalize legally your wishes for your children's

DO YOU WANT TO KNOW...

The Six Common Mistakes Most Parents (And Their Lawyers Make) When It Comes To Naming Guardians?

SCAN The QR Code To Make Sure You Don't Make One!

care as soon as possible. Friends, children do not belong in courtrooms. They belong in loving, safe environments where they are cared for and know how much God loves them. Don't let inaction leave your children at risk one more day. Let me encourage you to legally name permanent guardians for your children and to identify additional adults who can help support your guardians in this responsibility.

Chapter 3
SHORT-TERM CARE PLAN

If something unexpected happens to you, that means it was, well . . . unexpected! Most parents, and even most attorneys, don't give enough thought to what should happen during the initial emergency period after something has happened to the parents. They tend to focus only on the long term after a parent has died.

When parents come to my office for a first meeting, I ask them a single question: What will happen today to your kids if you don't make it home from this meeting? This question usually triggers a deer-in-the-headlights look and some panic. "Well, um, let's see, my ah daughter's school has an emergency contact card, so they'll call my friend Patty and she'll pick her up."

I ask follow-up questions. "Ok, so then let's say it's getting late in the evening and Patty still hasn't been able to get in touch with you?" That's when they realize Patty has no idea how to get in touch with relatives, and they start to throw out words like *police* and *hospitals.*

"So," they ask—and you may be wondering too, "what do the police do when they show up after getting a report that parents are missing?" They may just leave the kids in your friend's care but, typically, Child Protective Services (CPS) will be notified. Child Protective Services is a state agency that oversees the welfare of children. It usually becomes involved when parents are missing, or seriously injured, or die, and young children are left behind. It is a liability for them not to get involved once they are notified of such a situation.

The goal of CPS is to place children in a safe place, ideally in the care of their family members. However, CPS will not automatically leave your child with your babysitter or even your family member if you are missing or have died. This means that your children could be placed in temporary foster care—in the care of complete strangers—at the moment they need love and familiarity the most.

As this chart illustrates, temporary foster care can happen during the gap period between the time of your incapacity or death to the time a judge either appoints a temporary guardian, signs off on your choice for permanent guardians, or appoints a permanent guardian because you did not.

So, what can you specifically do today to keep this from happening in your family? You need to create a short-term care plan for your children that includes legal instructions regarding who gets notified if you're hurt or pass away, who can immediately take custody of your children, and who can make medical decisions for children if you cannot.

Temporary Care for Your Children

Your short-term care plan should identify and authorize people you trust to temporarily care for your children during an emergency, so they will not have to be placed in temporary foster care.

Temporary guardians (also known as standby guardians) should be people you trust who you know would provide your children much love and comfort during a crisis. We usually recommend that parents name at least four or five temporary guardians in case one or more are not available to help. Temporary guardians should live within twenty minutes so they can quickly get to the children during an emergency.

As an estate planning attorney and as a mom, I can tell you that **temporary foster care is the NUMBER ONE concern parents have when I ask them what bothers them the most about not having an estate plan**. It bothers them more than their money being tied up in court, it bothers them more than taxes, and it bothers them more than not having made their own medical wishes known. The fear of temporary foster care can be alleviated simply by naming temporary guardians through the proper legal documentation.

Children's Medical Directives

Back when my siblings and I were very young and our parents would go on a trip, they would compose a handwritten note outlining that whoever was caring for us in their absence could get medical care for us if we got hurt. Well, thanks to lawyers a simple handwritten note is not going to suffice for the hospitals.

Children need official legal medical directives that authorize other trusted adults to make their medical decisions in the parents' absence. Their medical directive should include who you authorize to make medical decisions on your behalf, and under what circumstances, and who you authorize to receive medical information about your child. These medical directives must comply with all necessary legal formalities to be valid.

Several years ago, there was a family in Los Angeles, California, involved in a fatal traffic collision. The parents were instantly killed and their baby was seriously injured. First responders rushed the injured infant to a local hospital and immediately placed her under the care of Child Protective Services. Several major medical procedures were performed on her at the direction of strangers who had no idea what the parents' wishes were for their daughter's treatment or care.

Now of course we are grateful to first responders and authorities who are willing to step in and assist our children, especially in a situation like this. However, most of us would prefer that our own trusted family members or dear friends would direct our children's medical care in our absence and according to our personal wishes and beliefs. That's why it's imperative that parents complete medical directives so decisions can be made by who they have chosen.

We will talk later about the type of care that Jesus wants for every one of us.

Alert System

Completing legal forms that authorize others to temporarily care for your kids and make their medical decisions during an emergency is not enough. There needs to be an alert system in place so these decision makers can be immediately notified.

First, parents should make sure that their temporary guardians and children's medical decisionmakers have a copy of the legal documentation they will need to step in and act. Both Child Protective Services (and eventually a court) will need this legal documentation before allowing them to act. Next, you will also want to ensure that you have a family emergency card in your wallet, so first responders know who you are, and who you want to be contacted if there's an emergency. And finally, you will also want to make sure that you have instructions displayed at your home for any caregivers, so they know what to do in an emergency, including who to contact.

Let me encourage you to get a short-term care plan in place right away. Don't let the prospect of these scenarios or the lack of a perfect option keep you from protecting your children and securing their future.

Chapter 4

PASSING ON YOUR MONEY

We've all heard the expression "you can't take it with you." Our home, our money, our business, our assets, and even our favorite watch or ring all get left behind. In the legal world, we collectively call these things *your estate*. So how do you pass your estate on to the individuals or charities you wish to benefit, and in the most efficient and protective way possible?

If you do not set up your own estate plan, then you are relying on your state's default methods for passing on your estate to others. And, as you'll discover, these methods are all problematic and create a serious risk that your estate will not ultimately go to others the way you (or God for that matter!) might have intended.

Option One: Joint Ownership

One way for you to pass your estate on to someone else is to own the asset jointly with them while you are alive, so it will automatically pass to them when you die, and vice versa.

For example, if you and your spouse are both listed as joint account holders on your checking account, the money will automatically pass to the survivor of you when the first of you passes away. Likewise, if the deed for your home lists both you and your spouse as joint owners of your home, then the home will automatically pass to the survivor of you when the first of you dies.

In the legal world, we describe this type of arrangement for holding assets as **joint ownership**. While this type of arrangement may seem ideal because everything can pass automatically, it can be very bad in reality. Here's why.

When you or the other person dies, all the money passes to the other person outright, without any restrictions or protections. This means the other person can give your share of the money away to anyone they want, such as a new friend, new spouse, or business partner, with no guarantee it will eventually go to the children when the surviving spouse dies. It also means that if your surviving spouse gets sued, or divorced, or faces a lawsuit later in life, the money you left behind for them can be taken away by these third parties. And finally, eventually the other joint account holder will die, and unless they did their estate planning by then, all that money (or whatever is left of it) is going to end up in the hands of the court system before going to your surviving spouse's next of kin (which by the way, could include a new spouse and other children).

Option Two: Designated Beneficiaries

Another way you can pass money on to someone else is to name them as a beneficiary on an account or policy so the money automatically goes to them upon your death. If you have a life insurance policy or a retirement account, you probably remember listing a beneficiary, which is the person the money will go to when you die. If you are like most people, you probably named your spouse as the primary beneficiary and your children as your backup or contingent beneficiary (if you listed a backup at all).

Passing money this way poses all the same problems you face when money passes through joint ownership. The money passes with no protections or restrictions, meaning your beneficiary can give the money away to whomever they want, and have it taken away by creditors, predators, lawsuits, and a new spouse. There is no guarantee the money you leave behind will ever make it to your children.

Even more problematic is if you name a minor child as a beneficiary. Because that child is not yet eighteen, a court would have to step in and set up all the necessary safeguards and protections a minor must have before giving access to the money, assuming you did not do this yourself.

Last, your family could face a huge problem if you have not kept your beneficiary designations up-to-date. We read about this all the time—a man dies, for example, and his wife discovers that his 401(k) had an ex-wife listed as a beneficiary. Or only one child was listed as a beneficiary and the account was not updated to include subsequently born children.

There are many potential problems when naming beneficiaries of your accounts. I will show you in Chapter 6 how you need to designate your beneficiaries so the money will pass to them the right way.

Option Three: Probate Court

The third option for passing money to someone else, assuming it did not automatically pass to another joint account holder or adult beneficiary, is for it to pass through probate court. This is your state's default plan for your estate if you did not successfully pass it on through other means.

So, what exactly is probate court? Probate court is a government-established court process that your estate will likely pass through before it can go on to someone else. Oftentimes money passed through joint ownership or beneficiary designations ends up in probate court eventually when the second spouse dies or when money was left directly to a minor.

Probate court is often described as a lawsuit you file against yourself and use your own money to pay for. While the thought of probate court sounds outrageous and people don't like it, 70% of all families will end up there.

I'll show you in the next chapter how to make sure your family is not one of them.

Chapter 5

AVOID PROBATE AT ALL COSTS!

If you have not yet experienced probate court for a loved one who has passed, I can assure you it's a miserable process. Here is what your family can expect, give or take, depending on the state you live in:

- Probate is a very long court process—it can even last two years or more depending on the state you live in and whether there's any family contention.

- Your money is frozen and is not immediately accessible for funeral costs and those financially dependent on you.

- Probate court is open and public, meaning anyone can go down to the court and see exactly what and how much you owned at the time of your death.

- Someone must open probate for your estate, and it may not be the person you would have wanted or chosen. This person is stuck cleaning up your mess. Imagine that—you die unexpectedly, and your family must not only deal with your loss, but also get thrown into the court system.

- Unless you had a valid will that directed otherwise, only your "legal next of kin" will inherit from you. This will be your spouse if you're married, and also your children, but only if they are related to you through blood or adoption. Stepchildren or other persons you consider as family are excluded. If you are unmarried and have no children, your next of kin is your beneficiary (typically parents, then siblings, then nieces and nephews), regardless of whether you had a close relationship with them while you were living. Your next of kin never includes the church or charities you may have supported.

- Probate court is depressing, as are most courtrooms. The halls are packed with people who are experiencing tremendous anxiety and grief as they await a cold courtroom to sort out their fate.

- Probate court is a platform for your family members to publicly air their grievances at one another.

- And finally, probate court is very, very, and I mean VERY expensive.

What Probate Costs

The cost of probate varies depending on the state you live in and oftentimes the size of your estate. In states like California where I live (hey now, at least we have great weather), the probate code sets the cost for probate as a percentage of the total value of your estate. This percentage of your estate pays the attorney and the person administering your estate. On top of that there are court fees, costs, and sometimes additional attorney's fees. We estimate for our clients that probate will cost them on average 5% of their total estate worth (it could be less or more depending on the size and complexity of the estate).

Let me give you a simple scenario to help explain what probate could cost your family. Here is a typical estate:

- Your Home: Your home has a market value of $500,000.

- Your Bank and Savings Accounts: You have about $15,000 in checking and $30,000 in savings.

- Your Stock: You have $50,000 worth of stock.

- Your Retirement Accounts: Your 401(k) has about $120,000. Your spouse does not have a 401(k).

- Your Life Insurance: You have a $1 million policy, and your spouse has a $250,000 policy.

- Your Debt: You still owe $200,000 on your mortgage, $60,000 in loans that helped finance college, and $15,000 on your Visa.

When the Probate court determines the value of this couple's estate, they are going to base the value only on the fair market value of each asset, and not offset it at all with the debt. This means for the couple I described above, their total estate worth would be as follows:

Asset	Fair Market Value
Home	$500,000
Checking & Savings	$45,000
Stock	$50,000
Retirement Accounts*	$120,000
Combined Life Insurance*	$1,250,000
Total Estate Worth:	$1,965,000
Your Probate Cost (at 5%)	*$98,250*

That's crazy, right? The probate cost for this couple who passed away is $98,250. That's a lot of money that could have gone to something or some*one* better.

How Life Insurance and Retirement Accounts Are Brought into Probate Court

We talked earlier about what happens when someone is named as the beneficiary on a life insurance policy or retirement account—the money goes to them outright without any restrictions or protections. If you have minor children listed as beneficiaries, the money will be brought into the probate case as children cannot receive any money outright until they are age eighteen.

If you don't have minor children, you can remove the life insurance and retirement accounts from the figures above. However, we've found that, for most families whose kids are grown or don't have children, their estate value tends to be larger than the figures in the example. You can substitute your own numbers to see how probate can indeed be very expensive!

Probate Lasts Even Longer If You Have Minor Children or If It Is Contested

If you have minor children, the nightmare of probate will continue until your youngest child is eighteen. This is true because the court usually will place whatever money is left (after the lawyers, courts, and fees are all paid) into court supervised accounts for each minor child. Every other year the appointed custodians/guardians of the account must go back to court to show how the money is being used for the benefit of the children. Once the children turn eighteen, they get whatever is left in their account, outright, without any restrictions.

Also, if your estate is contested in any way, meaning someone steps up and claims that he or she should be included when they weren't, or family members argue over your mental capacity when you made a will, or family members or creditors claim you owed them money and your next of kin disagrees, then court can sadly drag on for years. And I mean years!

What Happens after Probate Is Completed

If probate sounds like a nightmare, well it really is. Even when it comes to an end, it can leave an emotional scar on the family.

I knew a very tight-knit Catholic family with several adult children, one of whom was a single parent who had lived with the parents. The siblings remained tight with each other when their mom died but fell apart when the dad passed away a few years later. Dad had taken time to make a will at some point, but it was old and outdated when he passed away and had boilerplate language that didn't seem to really reflect the family's situation. In the will, Dad split everything equally among his children which seemed be straightforward and typical, other than the fact that the single adult child and the grandchild lived with Dad in the family home.

Half of the siblings strongly believed that Dad would have wanted the adult child and grandchild to remain living in the family home, at least until the grandchild was raised. The other half of the siblings felt that it was time for the adult child and grandchild to move

PROBATE NIGHTMARE

If your estate is contested in **ANY** way... court can sadly drag on for **YEARS.**

out and use their share of the inheritance to secure their own residence. This family battled with each other in probate court, and when all was said and done, hardly anyone in the family was talking. Even years later now, that family has never fully reconciled. If you think their story is the exception, sadly, it is not. It is all too common for families who don't have a complete plan in place.

Are you leaving your family in a situation like this? By not planning, or by having poor planning, are you subjecting your family to the expense and hassle and heartache of probate court? I can assure you as a professional who has seen countless families go through probate that the nature of the process itself can divide families—*good* families!

And remember, probate will cost a lot more than just time and money and strained relationships. It can often cost the person who died their reputation, as no one wants to be remembered as the person who died and left their family with a mess on their hands. This is not the outcome your family deserves.

Chapter 6

THE **BEST WAY** TO **PASS DOWN YOUR MONEY**

What if there was a better way to pass your money on to the people you love and the causes you care about? What if your loved ones could be spared from the awful nightmare of probate court? What if your money could immediately be used for your funeral expenses and your loved ones' support instead of a big chunk going to the government? And what if you could help avoid family drama and demonstrate your character as a responsible and loving family member? If you are like the rest of us, you are probably wondering how to make this possible.

The good news is that there is an escape from probate court! In fact, probate is completely voluntary—your loved ones end up there only if you choose for them to be there by your failure to act now.

You can prevent your loved ones from experiencing the grueling process of probate and its devastating effects by setting up a revocable living trust. In the legal world,

LAURA K. MEIER, ESQ.

we describe a revocable living trust as a legal agreement you create that governs how, upon your death, your assets will pass to the people or charities you've designated. Your trust is your way of saying, *this is who I am, this is who I love, this is who I want my money to go to and on what terms, and this is who I trust to be in charge of everything, so a judge doesn't have to get involved.*

If a revocable living trust sounds a lot like a will, well it is! Both legal documents formalize your wishes regarding the distribution of your assets upon your death. However, there is one major distinction—a will does not prevent your family from having to go through that long and expensive probate court process, but rather instructs a judge of your wishes. Only a revocable living trust can avoid the actual probate process itself (and the associated costs).

When I explain how a trust works to clients, I tell them to think of an empty box. We call that empty box your trust. Now think of everything you own—your home, your bank accounts, your investment accounts, your personal belongings, anything that is yours. Visualize yourself placing all these things inside that empty box. Now let's say that you get a new couch or buy a new property down the road, well you can add that to everything else inside that box. And let's say you sell a couch or sell a property, well that automatically then goes outside of the box.

When you pass away, a lid gets placed on top of the box. Anything inside of the box will privately and automatically get passed on according to your wishes from your trust.

However, anything left outside of the box ends up in probate (we will soon discuss how to make sure all of your money and assets get properly connected to your trust).

Creating a trust is a very easy way to make sure that your estate will privately and efficiently pass on to your loved ones or beloved charities rather than getting tied up in probate court for years. If a trust sounds a lot like magic, it is! And here is the best part—remember the enormous cost of probate we discussed earlier? It's eliminated when you set up your own estate plan that includes a revocable living trust.

You are probably wondering, why doesn't everyone just go and set up a trust-based estate plan? **The number one reason most people do not set up an estate plan is because they procrastinate.** So many people convince themselves they'll get around to setting up an estate plan with a trust before year's end, or before their next vacation, or when they retire. . . you may even have your own good reason for putting it off or not updating the one you have. (Don't worry, I am not judging you! I have my own "to-do" list!)

Or, sometimes even worse, people do take the time to set up an estate plan but fail to do it correctly. For example, they may have downloaded generic forms from the internet or used a discounted legal service, only for their loved ones to later discover that the plan doesn't work. Or, their loved one took time to get a "good plan" in place, but then failed to adequately update it throughout the years. Or, they failed to properly connect their assets to their trust, which we will talk about more a little later. These common missteps lead to families ending up in probate court, the exact situation that their loved one had hoped to avoid for them.

Here is the hard truth: life does happen, people do die, and I bet most people who died without having a sufficient estate plan thought they would take care of it before it was too late. How many of us realized when Covid hit that we did not have the legal, financial, or medical protections in place that we should have? How many families who lost loved ones during that crisis could not even turn to the courts for help because they were shut down? How many loved ones sat outside hospitals holding up signs, unable to advocate for their loved one's medical care by their bedside? What other monstrous wake-up call are we waiting for to motivate us to act and create a plan for our family?

Make sure your loved ones can avoid probate and that assets can be transferred painlessly and privately, by establishing a revocable living trust and keep it up to date. If you have a plan already that you suspect was done incorrectly or it's been some time since you've revisited it, please talk with your attorney right away and make the necessary changes.

Chapter 7

CHOOSING YOUR
BENEFICIARIES

When you say no to your state's default plan for probate and instead commit to creating a revocable living trust, it's like being handed a beautiful white canvas board on which you can create the vision for your assets and loved ones long after you're gone. Your trust can reflect your dream—and God's dream—for the gifts you've been given and the people you love.

You may be surprised to learn that the Catholic Church does not provide direct instruction regarding how one should distribute their assets upon their death. However, if you share the viewpoint that what we do in death should be an extension of what we do—or *should be doing*—in life, then we can draw much guidance from Catholic teachings regarding the proper use and disposition of assets, including our moral obligations as good stewards to our loved ones and the greater good.

We can begin this conversation by asking ourselves how we acquired our assets in the first place. How did you acquire your assets? If you asked me that, I'd probably tell you that I became a lawyer, worked at a big law firm, then started my own law firm, built up my clientele, hired more staff, saved and invested profits, and so on. You might have a similar story about how you labored to earn what you have.

But in the Letter of James, we are told, "Do not be deceived, my beloved brothers. All good giving and every perfect gift is from above, coming down from the Father of lights, within whom there is no alteration or shadow caused by change."[16] Our homes, our cars, our brokerage accounts, our businesses, our clothes, vacations—all of it comes from God.

The Catechism reminds us that although God has given us these gifts, we are obligated to use them for the greater good, and not only for personal benefit. "The right to private property, acquired or received in a just way, does not do away with the original gift of the earth to the whole of mankind. The **universal** destination of goods remains primordial, even if the promotion of the common good requires respect for the right to private property and its exercise."[17] Here, we are told that our assets are ultimately intended for the common good, and not just for ourselves or our own family.

16   James 1:16-17
17   Catechism 2403

This is not to suggest that we cannot use these God given gifts on ourselves or our own family while we are living, or in death. To the contrary, the Catechism reminds us that our first obligation is to our family members. "The ownership of any property makes its holder a steward of Providence, with the task of making it fruitful and communicating its benefits to others, first of all his family."[18] It's good to take care of our own family!

We are further instructed that not only is it good, but it is also our duty. Specifically, "the fourth commandment (to honor thy father and mother) reminds grown children of their responsibilities toward their parents. As much as they can, they must give them material and moral support in old age and in times of illness, loneliness, or distress."[19] We are also obligated as parents of young children to "provide for their physical and spiritual needs."

Once we meet our moral obligations to our own family members, we are warned not to use or consume the excess, but to "employ them in ways that will benefit the greatest numbers, reserving the **better part** for guests, for the sick and the poor."[20] Christ said, "Do not store up for yourselves treasures on earth...but store up treasures in heaven...for where your treasure is, there also will be your heart."[21]

---

18   Catechism 2404

19   Catechism 2218

20   Catechism 2405

21   Matthew 6:19-21

45

Keeping this guidance in mind, we can ask ourselves important questions like who am I morally obligated to leave money to and am I also considering the greater good? The good news is that when you create a revocable living trust, you get to decide how your estate will be distributed, honoring God's dream for your assets. We will look below on how to best pass assets to who you may intend to benefit.

As a reminder, when you fail to create your own plan for these assets, your state's default plan will apply, and the probate court won't consider any of your moral obligations as good stewards over your assets.

In addition to these moral obligations, we must also comply with our legal obligations. Creditors must be paid, and in most circumstances, spouses and minor/dependent children cannot be legally disinherited. Beyond that, the law allows you to legally distribute your assets how you see fit. There is no legal right in the United States for adult children to inherit from their parents, or visa versa.

> "Who am I morally obligated to leave money to and am I also considering the **GREATER GOOD?**"

Let's look now on how to best pass money on to specific beneficiaries you will likely include, meeting both your moral and legal obligations to them and to the common good.

Chapter 8

PASSING MONEY TO YOUR SPOUSE

Many spouses own their assets jointly and intend for the surviving spouse to retain control of the money when the first spouse dies. This way, the surviving spouse can continue to have the resources they need for themselves, the family, and to benefit the greater good. There are also legal and tax considerations where it is favorable to choose your surviving spouse as your beneficiary.

There are certain situations where one might forego leaving their money to their surviving spouse, like in situations where there is a remarriage, and the spouses wish to leave their respective estates to their own children. If you are not planning on leaving your money to your surviving spouse, you will want to consult with both a family law attorney and an estate planning attorney to confirm that this "plan" is legally permissible.

If you choose to leave money to your surviving spouse, doing so through a trust will avoid probate and ensure their uninterrupted support. You can also create certain restrictions and protections over the money you are leaving them in trust so it will eventually trickle down to secondary beneficiaries you've chosen after your surviving spouse dies.

There are two popular options for passing money through your trust to your spouse. Option one allows you to pass the money to your spouse outright where they can retain complete control over the assets. Option two includes certain protections and restrictions over the assets. Let's look at both and see what's best for you and your spouse.

Option One: Giving Your Spouse the Money Free and Clear

Many people like the concept of leaving the money to their spouse outright, free of any restrictions (and protections). In the legal world, we call this the **Disclaimer Method**. The disclaimer method is very similar to passing your money through joint ownership or naming your spouse as the beneficiary on a policy or account. It allows for extreme flexibility since your spouse receives your share of the money with "no strings attached."

The downside is that the surviving spouse can do whatever they want with your share of the assets, and they have the exclusive say over how it is managed and spent. They can also give it away to a new spouse or someone other than your children. They could also risk losing it if they are later sued, divorced, or preyed upon.

Option Two: Giving Your Spouse Money with Restrictions and Protections

You may really like the idea of the surviving spouse having control over all the assets but you may not necessarily want them to have the power to spend it however they want or the power to disinherit children. You also may want to protect your spouse from the risk of losing the money to ill-intentioned third parties.

There are several techniques that attorneys can use to provide for this type of protection, but the technique I generally prefer to use is called the **Clayton Election**. The Clayton Election allows a spouse to leave money behind for the continued support of the surviving spouse (including health, education, maintenance, and support), but restricts them from using the money for other purposes, like paying off creditors or judgments, or giving it away to people other than the beneficiaries you both agreed upon. They can use the income from the trust for whatever they want.

Many couples are less concerned about their spouse doing something bad with the money and more concerned it could be lost to ill-intentioned third parties. They want their spouse to have lots of flexibility in how the money is used, but don't want them to give it away or have it taken from them.

This type of arrangement is called a **beneficiary controlled asset protection trust**. I really like this setup because you are essentially giving your surviving spouse complete control, yet protecting that money from ill-intentioned third parties. They will have many options for protecting that money if they are ever facing a divorce, lawsuit, bankruptcy, creditor, or any other outside threat. You can also give your spouse a **limited power of appointment**, which would allow them the option for including a gift to charity upon their death.

What's best for you and your spouse largely depends on your goals and family situation. Working with a well-respected estate planning attorney highly knowledgeable in asset protection trusts and tax laws can help you make the best decision for your family.

Chapter 9
PASSING MONEY TO YOUR CHILDREN

Many people wish to leave their money to their children, typically after the surviving spouse dies. It's important that you know your options so you can responsibly pass down your assets to them.

A few years ago I met with a young woman who had just had her first son. I asked what brought her in to get her estate planning in place, assuming she'd say guardianship, but for her, that wasn't it. She said, "I'm here because I never want to burden my son with money."

I was thinking, *That sounds like a great problem to have!*

But it wasn't. She told me that when she was eighteen years old, she received a very large inheritance, outright and without any restrictions. She was extremely bright, but instead of going to college as she had planned and doing all the things most of us do in our twenties to build our futures, she ended up traveling and attracting the wrong people. It all came to halt when she found out she was expecting a child. By the time she came in to see me, all the money was gone. She was starting over from scratch. She taught me an important lesson:

Passing money to your children at the wrong time (too young), and in the wrong way (without restrictions) creates a burden for them rather than a blessing.

I know you would never want your children to experience the pain and heartache our client did because of sudden wealth. The good news is that you can keep this from happening by passing money through a trust that is properly structured and managed. A trust allows you to create the terms for how you want to provide for your children and who you want to manage the money on their behalf until they come of the appropriate age.

There are three popular types of beneficiary trusts that you will likely want to use: common trusts, stated age trusts, and lifetime asset protection trusts.

Common Trusts

If you have more than one child and they are all under eighteen, it makes a lot of sense to keep your money for them all together to be used for their health, education, maintenance, and support. This type of structure, which the legal world calls a **common trust**, allows the adult in charge of the money (the trustee) to draw from one shared pot of money. It mirrors what we are doing now for our children while we are alive, as one child one month might soak up more money than their siblings, then visa versa.

At some point, after the kids are raised and become more independent, the common trust should end. You can decide the appropriate age for that to happen, at which point the remaining money will be divided up and transferred into separate trusts for each child, which we'll look at below. We usually recommend the common trust terminate when the youngest turns eighteen, or, if the family is college-minded, then when the youngest turns twenty-four or graduates from college, whichever occurs first.

Stated Age Trusts

After the common trust terminates, the remaining assets can be divided into separate **stated age trusts** for each of your children. While the assets are in the separate trusts, your trustee will use the assets for your children's benefit. But when each child reaches certain ages or milestones, you can instruct the trustee to distribute all or a portion of the trust assets to your child outright without restrictions. You can do this all-in-one lump sum or you can distribute a percentage of the trust assets at stated ages (e.g., at age twenty-five the child gets 25% of the trust assets, at age thirty the child gets 50% of the trust assets, and at age thirty-five the child gets the remaining trust assets).

For those who still have kids under age 30 give or take, you might be wondering what's the right age to give your adult children full access to their inheritance? Some things to consider are:

- The trust always pays for your child's health, education, maintenance, and support, so really what you're determining is at what age you want your child—rather than the adult who was put in charge of the money—to control the money and spend it.

- Brain development does not end until age twenty-five.

- People experience many platonic and romantic relationships in their twenties, and many of your child's peers will not yet have their own money and success in their twenties. You don't want your child to stand out as the "rich kid" and thus attract people to them for the wrong reasons. Hopefully, once your child and their peers hit their thirties, they will all be on more equal footing since their peers will have become more self-sufficient and settled down.

- The twenties is a time when people develop tremendously (at lease it should be!). You don't want money waiting in the wings to deter your children from graduating from college and establishing their own career and independence.

As you can see, I am not a big fan of beneficiaries getting full access to their money in their twenties. Clients usually ask, what about a wedding, or starting a business, or a home? You can structure your trust to allow the trustee of your child's money to use trust money to pay for these important things and anything else you want; it just means that the trustee gets to use discretion on what amount is appropriate for these purposes, rather than giving your child free reign.

Once your child hits the age you've chosen for them to receive their money, the money is fully theirs, outright and clear. This means they can spend it, lose it, invest it, use it on other people, or give it away however they want. The assets are also subject to creditors, predators, and divorce.

Lifetime Asset Protection Trusts

The **lifetime asset protection trust** allows you to provide for your child's health, education, maintenance, support, and anything else you allow, but, unlike the stated age trust, the money stays protected in the trust for your child's lifetime. The power of the lifetime asset protection trust is that the money is always available for your child's benefit, but it is protected from improper or wasteful spending and from the outside world (e.g., creditors, predators, and divorce).

Whether we like it or not, divorce and lawsuits are prevalent in society today. All of us are at risk of third-party threats. A lifetime asset protection trust is one of the few options available to protect a child's inheritance against the outside world. This is the type of trust I have chosen for my own children.

There are two ways to set up a lifetime asset protection trust for your child.

One option is to make a trustee in charge of the money for your child's entire lifetime, so while the child benefits from the money, they never actually control it. Some clients don't like the idea because they feel it is too controlling. Other clients, who already know that their children will never become responsible enough to manage their own money or struggle with addiction, like this arrangement.

The other option is to set up the trust so your child will always benefit from the trust, but at some point will get to control it as well. Many people find this arrangement ideal because it provides their child both freedom and protections.

I also encourage my clients to create **lifetime trust distribution guidelines**, which provide further guidance and instruction to your trustee on how you would like your assets to be used for your child. This can include your vision and encouragement for them to pursue their education, career opportunities, maintain family relationships, or engage in philanthropic endeavors—anything good you'd like to encourage them to do. The idea is that these guidelines can provide the same support and encouragement to your child that you would if you were still alive.

On that note, the Catechism is very clear on our duties as parents not only to young children, but also to our adult children. "When they become adults, children have the right and duty to choose their profession and state of life. They should assume their new responsibilities within a trusting relationship with their parents, willingly asking and receiving their advice and counsel. Parents should be careful not to exert pressure on their children either in the choice of a profession or in that of a spouse. This necessary restraint does not prevent them—quite the contrary—from giving their children judicious advice, particularly when they are planning to start a family." Keeping these principles in mind, we should leave instructions behind in our lifetime distribution guidelines that serve as guidance for our children, and not as pressure from the grave or as conditions for receiving their inheritance.

The best trust for your child is the one that sets your child up for success. I encourage you to talk with an attorney who has a lot of experience in this area who can guide you into making the best decision for your child.

Chapter 10

PROVIDING FOR CHILDREN WITH DISABILITIES

If you have a child or a grandchild with a disability, you will need to pass their inheritance to them in a special way, so as not to disrupt their eligibility for current or future government benefits they may be entitled to. This is typically done through a **special needs trust**.

It used to be that many well-intentioned parents or grandparents would disinherit their child with a disability from their will or trust, knowing that such a gift would render them ineligible for government benefits. Instead, they would leave the money to an adult sibling or someone else they trusted to voluntarily use the money for the benefit of the child with a disability. This proved to be a failed approach, as the money often would get lost to the trusted custodian's own creditors, or divorces, or passed on to others when the custodian of the funds died rather than the child with the disability.

The good news is that you can legitimately pass money to your child with a disability through a special needs trust. A special needs trust is a special kind of trust that can hold your assets for the benefit of your child with a disability, without rendering them ineligible for current or future government benefits.

Pope Francis reminds us that "Every human person is precious and has value that does not depend on what they have or on their abilities, but on the simple fact that he or she is a person, the image of God...If disability or illness makes life more difficult, it is no less worthy of being lived and lived to the fullest...Our fellow human beings with disabilities must be at the center of our care and concern."[22]

One great way to ensure your child with special needs can live life to the fullest, in addition to having the resources they will need through their government benefits and special needs trust, is for you as their parent or conservator to create a **Memorandum of Intent**. This legal document allows you to outline your child's emotional needs and provide your insight to guide future caretakers in how to meet these needs. From ensuring the funds you've left them can be used to help facilitate their religious and social activities, to where you wish for them to live, to who you want to remain active in their life, you can outline the vision you have for your loved one.

---

22   Pope Francis statement in Paul VI Hall on Dec. 13, 2021

Setting up a special needs trust is very complex, and only some estate planning lawyers work within this specialty. Be sure you are working with a reputable attorney who focuses on this unique area of law. Additionally, you will probably need to consult with a professional who can help you secure any government benefits your child may be entitled to because of their disability.

MEMORANDUM OF INTENT outlines your child's emotional needs and guides future caretakers in how to meet these needs.

Chapter 11

PASSING MONEY TO OTHER FAMILY MEMBERS

Many people choose to include other family members or godchildren in their estate plan. We talked earlier about our moral obligation to care for our elderly parents "as much as we can, and to give our parents material and moral support in old age and in times of illness, loneliness, or distress." I can share with you countless touching stories of adult children, of all different beliefs and backgrounds, who care for their elderly parent, or include a gift for them through a trust or beneficiary designation to ensure their parent would have enough money for their care if something unexpectedly should happen to the adult child. I can also share with you a handful of sad stories where an elderly parent is left alone without any family support.

When you set up your estate plan, you will have the option of leaving a gift to anyone you wish to benefit, including your aging parents. If you are currently supporting your parents now or anticipate that you likely will be called to in their old age, then it's important to ensure that your estate can set aside the necessary resources for this expenditure without impeding your financial, legal, and moral obligations to your own spouse or children. If there are not enough resources for all, many adult children will consider obtaining a life insurance policy on themselves to ensure their estate can satisfy the needs of everyone dependent on them.

Most adult children who choose to leave their parent money identify a specific amount for the gift. You have the option to leave the gift outright to them without restrictions, or through a trust where it can be used for their basic support with any remaining funds at the end of their lifetime going back to your other dependent family members (i.e. your spouse and children). You will want to talk with your attorney on what structure is best for making such a gift which will largely depend on your circumstances and goals.

Chapter 12

BENEFITING THE COMMON GOOD

We talked earlier about God's call for us to be good stewards of the gifts He has given us, to reserve the better part for others, and our duty to care for both our family members and the common good. Let's further explore now and identify how God is specifically calling you to act on His behalf.

I am reminded of a visit a few years ago to the Women in the Military exhibit at Arlington Cemetery in Washington D.C. I listened to a recording from an interview with a former military nurse who had served in the Vietnam war. She recounted how difficult her service was because of the mass horror she witnessed, so much so that she felt God had abandoned His children there. She said that when she returned home to the U.S., she felt deeply depressed and had "lost her faith in God and in humanity."

A year or so later, a fellow nurse who had served alongside her came to visit her. When she told her how dark and angry she still felt and how she felt God had abandoned His children, her friend said something that really changed her perspective: "Did it ever occur to you that maybe God was present in Vietnam, working through *you*?" This new perspective restored her faith, changed her life, and helped heal her broken heart.

Friends, God often does his best work in the world through the living hands of human beings. While very few of us will ever be called to serve on the front lines of a war, or give our last penny to another, God is counting on all of us, in our own unique ways, to use our time, talents, and treasures to do His work in the world. Each day, we should wake up with a sense of purpose, asking God to direct our steps and to help us to see who He is calling us to help. We should continually ask God to instill in us a spirit of abundance and generosity.

As I personally reflect alongside you on how God is asking us to share the many gifts He has given us, I am asking myself, and you may be asking too—*How much is enough, for my own family, and for the common good?* For whatever reason, this question often seems to trigger in many a feeling of scarcity, even for those who have money! It can trigger a false belief that resources are fixed and limited, when in truth, God is the ultimate provider and will faithfully and continually replenish gifts (and bank accounts!). Just as God has provided for us, He will also continue to provide for our children, and our children's children, long after we are gone.

In the Gospel according St. Matthew, we are assured, "Do not worry and say, 'What are we to eat?' or 'What are we to drink?' or 'What are we to wear?' All these things the pagans seek. Your heavenly Father knows that you need them all. But seek ye first the kingdom of God and his righteousness and all these things will be given you besides." In this passage, God is telling us to ditch the scarcity mentality and that there is always more than enough for our own family and for the greater God, even when it comes to divvying up an inheritance.

As we think about the right amount to leave our family and the greater good, Catholic teachings can help us understand *how much* and *to whom*. No longer bound by the ten percent tithe from the Old Testament (although many dioceses still use this figure as a guide), we as Catholics are instead instructed "to give according to our means."[23] The Catholic Church proposes that we personally reflect on these four questions to help us determine how much to give to charity:

1. **Are my gifts to the common good *proportional* to what I have?** This is perhaps why the black and white rule of the ten percent tithe does not always make

---

23   Stewardship, A Disciples Response, Tenth Anniversary Edition, US Conference of Catholic Bishops, Page 67.

sense. For those who have so much, ten percent may simply not be enough. And for those who have so little, ten percent may simply be too much. To help you answer this question for yourself, you can add up the value of your estate, including insurance policies, to determine how much you would be leaving behind if you passed on today, and then ask if the amount you are considering leaving to the greater good is proportional to all that you have. One priest said he likes to suggest to families to treat the church just like an extra child, as that seems to keep things proportional. What great and practical advice!

2. **Have I actively *planned* as part of my monthly budget or estate plan to make a gift to the common good?** We all know that the best of intentions does not always equate to action. That's why we should formalize our intentions now regarding how much we will gift during our lives and in our deaths. Add into your budget now the monthly amount you will commit to donate, just like you factor in your electric bill or your grocery costs. That's how good intentions become actions—they are planned! You will also want to update your estate plan or beneficiary designation forms to include a proportional gift to the church or charities. That's the only way to ensure that gifts for the greater good can be made when you

pass away (aside from an estate tax, which we will talk about next).

3. **Is my charitable giving *prayerful*?** Every one of us should ask God through prayer where He is calling us to make a difference. God's calling for your life is unique and different from mine and others. I am reminded of the story of philanthropist Ronald Katz, who was so moved after seeing a tv news story about a marine, Aaron Mankin, who was disfigured from a roadside bombing, that Katz decided to help found UCLA Operation Mend to help heal wounded soldiers. Mankin became their first patient, followed by many others. Just as God moved Katz's heart for a very unique purpose, He will move yours too. Ask God through prayer to open your heart (and your wallet!) and for the courage to do the right thing.

4. **Is my charitable gift *sacrificial*?** Ooof. The word sacrifice. It seems like a lot, doesn't it? No one wants to go without. I know I don't. But, in the Gospel according to St. Matthew, we read about the power of sacrifice in the story of the widow who put her last two coins into the treasury, knowing she had no future financial support because of her husband's death. Jesus said, "Amen, I say to you, this poor widow put in more than all the other contributors to the treasury. For they have all contributed from their surplus wealth, but she, from her poverty, has contributed all

she had, her whole livelihood."[24] This story reminds us of God's desire for us to have a giving heart, and faith that He will always find a way to take care of our needs even when resources seem scarce. We can trust that when we give up something we *need* (not just out of our excess) for someone else who *needs it more*, that God will still find a way to provide for us. Sacrificial giving doesn't hurt—it actually makes you feel good and demonstrate your faith in God.

Friends, I believe that if we go through these questions, not just once, but often, we will have clarity on how much to give and to whom. Jesus Christ literally hung on the cross and gave up His life for us. In return, He is not even asking us to do the same or gift away our last penny. He is just asking us to please share some of the many gifts He has faithfully given us to be part of His work in this world. It should excite us, not terrify us, that we might have the exact gifts that He needs to perform miracles on earth today.

God might be calling you today to leave a gift behind for your local diocese to care for the retired clergy, feed the poor, or help educate His children in the faith. He might be calling you today to leave a gift behind for your alma mater, so a young person has a chance at an education or a meal before class. He might be calling you today to donate

---

24   Matthew 12:41-44

your old car to a local non-profit that helps children get the medical care their family cannot afford. Think carefully about what gifts you've been given, and how much should be gifted in life and in death. And don't be afraid to throw some cash in the second collection!

I know it can feel overwhelming sometimes when we look at the needs around us, and ask, will my gift even make a difference? But friends, our contributions, no matter how big or small, will absolutely make a difference. As Mother Teresa said, "Never worry about numbers. Help one person at a time and always start with the person nearest you." Imagine a doctor seeing an injured person in front of her and saying, my gift to heal others can't be used on everyone, so I won't even try to save the life in front of me. Of course not. Look left, look right, and ask God where He needs you to act.

I hope you are feeling more excited about sharing your time, your talents, and treasures. While most of us are familiar with how to give gifts to others while we are alive, many are unsure how to do this as their final act as well. Here are some ways you can leave a gift upon your death to help our fellow brothers and sisters in need:

- You can name the church or a charity as the beneficiary on your retirement account.

- You can name the church or a charity as a beneficiary on your life insurance policy.

- You can leave a specific gift in your will or trust to the church or a charity for a specific dollar amount, and even for a specific purpose.

- You can name the church or a charity as a residual beneficiary and leave a certain percentage of your estate.

- You can name the church or a charity as your "remote contingent beneficiary" so if your other beneficiaries should die with you or before you, then your estate can then go to the church or charity.

- You can donate real property to the church, typically gifted through your will or trust.

Once you identify those gifts you wish to make, I encourage you to contact the church and any other charitable organizations you included to let them know as this helps them for planning purposes. Also, don't let them just settle for getting your money! Become a face they will one day miss! Get involved today with the causes that God put in your heart and witness the miracles that happen through your generosity.

And one final note…Some of you, even if you don't feel compelled to leave a gift to the greater good as part of your final act, will be forced to through estate taxation. That's because you have a lot of, you know, money! Society will only allow you to pass on so much of that money without paying estate taxes. You can check with your attorney to find out how much you are legally allowed to pass down without estate taxes being triggered. The good news is that you can typically reduce your estate tax liability through charitable giving, and there are many estate planning strategies that can help you accomplish that.

READY TO MAKE A DIFFERENCE FOR THE GREATER GOOD?

Regardless of whether you feel motivated to leave a charitable gift because of an estate tax liability or just out of the goodness of your heart, the church and your other favorite charities will happily accept your gifts either way! Let's encourage one another to step up now in a spirit of gratitude and abundance to help continue God's work in this world.

One day, when we meet our maker, I pray that everyone of us will hear these words from our loving Savior in appreciation for answering His call:

"Come, you who are blessed by my father. Inherit the kingdom prepared for you from the foundation of the world. For I was hungry, and you gave me food, I was thirsty and you gave me drink, a stranger and you welcomed me, naked and you clothed me, ill and you cared for me, in prison and you visited me…Amen, I say to you, whatever you did for one of these brothers of mine, you did it for me."[25]

In case we were wondering some ways we should help, let's read that passage again. May God bless you and your family, and the generations to come, for your loving generosity and support.

---

25   Matthew 25:34-40

Chapter 13

THE #1 REASON TRUSTS FAIL

We've talked a lot now about why you should have a revocable living trust and how it can protect our assets and loved ones and help us do good in the world. You are probably getting excited about the idea of setting one up to benefit your loved ones and the greater good! But, I am going to have to take a little wind out of your sails because not all revocable living trusts work the way they needed to. In fact, many trusts fail.

Trusts fail for many different reasons, some of which I already alluded to. They weren't set up properly, they excluded rightful beneficiaries, they became outdated. However, **the number one reason that trusts fail is that people do not move their assets into their trust.**

Your assets will not automatically go into your trust just because you signed a legal document that said "trust" on it! Once your trust is created, you must start moving your assets into that trust and continue to do so every time you acquire a new asset (also known as "funding your trust"). Do not assume your attorney did or will do this for you.

I have personally seen individuals fail to:

- Change title on the deed to their home to the name of the trust.

- Change the account holder name on their banking and investment accounts to the name of the trust.

- Change the beneficiary of their life insurance policy to the name of the trust.

- Change the contingent beneficiary on their retirement account to the name of the trust.

In other words, they do not take the proper steps to put their stuff into the box! Thus, all the stuff left outside of the box ends up in probate.

Buyer beware! Never hire a law firm or anybody else to help you set up a trust if they are simply leaving it up to you to put your assets into it yourself. You won't! Half of my clients who come to me with a trust already set up discover that their attorney only *mentioned* to them they needed to do this, rather than doing it for them or guiding them through the process.

The **worst** calls I get are from people who just lost a loved one and thought that they had their estate planning all set up, only to discover that none of the assets were moved into the trust. They are crushed! They thought all along that this crucial task had been taken care of, only to discover it wasn't and there is now nothing they can do about it.

Make sure you take the proper steps to move your assets into your trust and to double check each year that they are still properly connected. Also make sure you seek individual legal guidance on how to properly title your assets or designate beneficiaries, as it's not a one size fits all application.

NEED HELP gathering all your assets in one place?

SCAN here to get a free family wealth inventory spreadsheet to help you organize your affairs.

Chapter 14
YOUR COMPLETE CARE DURING A MEDICAL CRISIS

A couple of years ago, when my oldest son Conrad was sixteen, he woke up one morning and could not see out of his left eye. Thinking it must be irritated, I told him to "go take a shower." But he was adamant about seeing a doctor. I got him in with his primary care physician that afternoon, who upon examining Conrad, said, "this is very serious." At first, I thought he was joking, but then he called his personal ophthalmologist and requested she see us immediately. "Go straight there and don't stop," he told us.

The ophthalmologist examined Conrad and told us it appeared that his retina had detached. She sent us immediately over to one the top surgeons in the country, Dr. Timothy You, who confirmed her findings and said Conrad needed emergency surgery or the vision loss could be permanent. For a mom expecting to pop into an urgent care that day and get my kid an antibiotic, you can imagine my shock upon hearing my son had gone blind!

As Conrad was being prepped for surgery the following morning, Dr. You came in to greet us and go over what to expect in the operating room. When he asked Conrad if he had any questions, Conrad said, "No, but I'm scared." I thought to myself, *I'm scared too. Will this surgery work? Will my son get his eyesight back? How did this even happen?*

Dr. You shook his head acknowledging my son's fear. "You're scared?" He said, compassionately. "Would you like me to pray with you?"

Those words, coming from Dr. You in that moment, felt like an unexpected gift from God. I could not believe that God not only led us to this renowned surgeon so quickly, but that he was also a man of faith. Dr. You proceeded to speak a beautiful prayer over my son, asking God to guide his hands and his team's hands in the operating room to help heal Conrad's eye and restore his vision.

Now, we all know, that even with the best medical care and great faith, that things don't always go as planned. What was supposed to be a one-hour surgery, turned into a four-hour surgery, and when Dr. You finally came out, I could tell by his demeanor that things weren't good. He immediately began drawing pictures and explaining that the tearing in Conrad's eye was more significant than they had anticipated, and that his eye had rejected the typical repair method. While he expressed confidence that his retina was successfully re-attached using an alternative method, he expressed concern about his vision returning.

"Will he *ever* be able to see?" I asked. Very truthfully, he said, "I don't know."

If you've ever received an uncertain or concerning medical prognosis, then you know, it's a lot to take in. Yet, as I processed what Dr. You was saying, I simultaneously felt a strange sense of peace and reassurance coming from within, knowing that Conrad had so many people who loved him and that God still had a beautiful plan for his life. I had a glimpse in my head of him very happy and thriving years in the future, surrounded by all our extended family. I also felt a strange sense of gratitude for the vision he still had in his other eye, knowing that would be a miracle for some parents to hear. I believe my thoughts and feelings were not entirely coming from me. It's as though I could feel the presence of God comforting me in that moment.

When I shared these thoughts out loud, Dr. You told me what a great comfort it was knowing Conrad was going home to all this family and love. "Many of my patients who need this type of surgery are very elderly and they go through this alone. They take taxis home because no one will even drive them. And I am very happy to know that your family has faith."

He then quoted me a verse from the Holy Bible that I would repeat over and over the following year, as Conrad's vision failed to return, and he faced more grueling surgeries with long recovery periods, that required he lay face down for weeks. "Romans 8:28," Dr. You said. "*All* things work together for good for those who love God, who are called according to his purpose. *All* meaning the good and the bad. So, I agree with you, that Conrad has a very bright future no matter his prognosis."

Do you know the distinction between a hope*ful* and hope*less* situation when a medical crisis occurs? *The presence of God.* He longs to comfort and sustain us in our time of need and assures us that He wants us to be healed. "For I the Lord am your healer."[26] The Holy Bible speaks of numerous accounts of Jesus being close to those with infirmities, praying for them, healing them, and even raising Lazarus from the dead. "Everyone in the crowds sought to touch him because power came forth from him and healed them all."[27] Jesus is indeed the ultimate healer and the giver of life.

Even when we are believing with great faith that we will be healed, but our physical bodies fail us, we can still have hope, because Jesus promises us that He will always heal our soul and bring us home to eternal life. "Even in the face of death—for many, a time when hope seems lost—the Church witnesses to her belief that God has created each person for eternal life."[28] For "God himself will always be with them [as their God]. He will wipe away every tear from their eyes, and

---

26   Exodus 15:26

27   Luke 6:19

28   Ethical and Religious Directives for the Catholic Health Care Services, Sixth Edition, page 20.

there shall be no more death or mourning, wailing or pain, for the old order has passed away."[29] God is so faithful in his love to us that He has even promised to raise us up on the last day.

With my son's situation, as our hope for his vision returning *decreased* as time passed on, our faith in God and his unfailing love *increased*. Not because we were getting the results we wanted, but because we could undeniably feel God's presence as evidenced by the excellent medical care Conrad received, the incredible support from family, friends, and his school, the amount of people praying, and a supernatural feeling of peace.

While it was hard to watch Conrad struggle to keep up with classes, say goodbye to sports that had been a huge part of his life, and delay milestones like getting his license, we were moved by his upbeat outlook. With each new obstacle or disappointment, he would say, "I can do all things through Christ which strengthens me." For a mother, I began to see how God was teaching Conrad to see with his spiritual eyes while his physical eye struggled. The bad things were indeed working together for good, just as his surgeon had promised.

Catholic teachings remind us that "for the Christian, our encounter with suffering and death can take on a positive and distinctive meaning through the redemptive power of Jesus' suffering and death. As St. Paul says, we are always carrying about the body of the dying of Jesus, so that the life

---

29   Revelations 21:3-4

of Jesus may also be manifested in our body. This truth does not lessen the pain and fear but gives confidence and grace for bearing suffering rather than being overwhelmed by it."[30] We can always maintain hope in our suffering when we acknowledge God's tender mercies and presence.

Just as we had accepted that Conrad's vision would never return, we were told that he needed one final surgery to retain the dark shadow vision he had regained from previous surgeries that was now being threatened by a cataract. We were told not to expect any improvement to the vision he now had. I can assure you it's no fun for a teenager, or anyone, having a surgery when you're told you should still expect a bad result!

But, we would soon discover that just as *bad things* can happen unexpectedly, that *good things* can too. When the bandages were removed following that surgery, Conrad yelled out, "I can see!" Our son's vision had miraculously returned, after a year from when it was first lost. His surgeon and other physicians called it a 'medical miracle'. Today, our son sees perfectly out of both of his eyes. Thanks be to God.

I can share with you also that Conrad continues to use his spiritual eyes when facing new life challenges—a special ability that somehow could only be taught to him from going through his vision challenge.

I know that, in an ideal world, none of us would have to go through great suffering to learn important lessons or

---

30   Ethical and Religious Directives for the Catholic Health Care Services, Sixth Edition, page 6

how to put our trust in God. Yet, we all know that, on a log-ical level, no one is exempt from life's inherent challenges, including you and me. How can we receive the best possible medical care and invite God to be present in our challenges if something unexpected happens?

As we turn now to discussing how you can best prepare for an unexpected medical crisis, we will not just focus on your *physical* care, but your *complete* care. "Jesus' healing mission went further than caring only for physical affliction. He touched people at the deepest level of their existence: he sought their physical, mental, and spiritual healing."[31]

This is the type of care that Jesus wants for you.

---

31   Ethical and Religious Directives for the Catholic Health Care Services, Sixth Edition, page 6.

Chapter 15

THE IMPORTANCE OF CREATING MEDICAL DIRECTIVES

One of the most important ways to ensure our complete care during a medical crisis is to have legal documents outlining our wishes. In the legal world, we call these type of legal documents **medical directives**. They serve as our voice if we are physically or mentally unable to advocate for ourselves. Without medical directives, your family members would be forced to go through a court process called a conservatorship that is costly and causes delays. You might also not receive the complete care you would have desired.

Medical directives cover things like who you trust to make your medical decisions, who your physicians can share your private medical information with, what type of procedures you are okay or not okay with, how you feel about certain life-sustaining procedures, and your wishes for your physical, spiritual, and mental care. Without comprehensive medical directives, you are leaving way too much to chance.

You might recall the Terri Schiavo case many years ago, when a young woman suffered a major brain injury rendering her completely unable to care for herself. Unfortunately, Terri did not have medical directives. For over a decade, her husband and parents battled in court with each other over what they believed her wishes were regarding life-prolonging procedures. Her husband argued she would not want continued life-sustaining procedures given her condition and prognosis, while her parents argued that she would because of her Catholic beliefs.

Terri's case was so highly publicized and contentious that it drew in multiple courts, the legislature, advocacy groups, and even the President of the United States. Ultimately, a court ordered that Terri's feeding tube be removed and she passed away soon after. The one thing everyone could seem to agree on in the end is how important it is to have medical directives to make your wishes known, and that no family should ever be put in that nightmare position of guessing or going through court.

Without comprehensive medical directives, you are leaving way TOO MUCH to chance.

When you complete your medical directives and hopefully avoid a heartbreaking situation like Terri's, you will want to ensure your wishes are grounded in both science and faith. Without one or the other, you cannot have the complete care that Jesus wants for you. "The dialogue between medical science and Christian Faith has for its primary purpose the common good of all persons. It presupposes that science and faith do not contradict each other. Both are grounded in respect for truth and freedom."[32]

However, not all medical directives are rooted in both science and faith. Some rely only on faith for healing, and reject modern medicines, technologies, and life-sustaining procedures. Other medical directives omit faith completely, and rely only on science, which often changes with new research, new technologies, new ethics, and new political influences. That's why we need to incorporate both—faith to help us navigate medical decisions with the wisdom from our God who "is the same, yesterday, today, and tomorrow", and science that allows God to heal us through physicians, modern medicine, technologies, and life-sustaining procedures within His boundaries for human life.

Catholic teachings remind us that our health care decisions are not ours alone to make but must be made according to God's will and boundaries for human life. Afterall, our bodies ultimately belong to Him, and we are to honor God with its use. "Do you not realize that your body is the temple of the holy spirit, who is in you and whom you received from God? You are not your own property, then; you have been

---

32   Ethical and Religious Directives for the Catholic Health Care Services, Sixth Edition, page 7

bought at a price. So, use your body for the glory of God."[33] This is why it is a tragedy when anyone, including our own self, intentionally uses or harms our body in a way that God did not intend.

We also believe as Catholics that God's standard of care for our human bodies is a much higher standard than the world's. While the world says we value human life, followed by *except if/when*, God instead puts a period. He doesn't base our inherent worth to Him on whether we can still do back flips or long division following a serious medical event. You are valuable to God no matter what and He wants the medical community to do what they can, within scientific and faith-based boundaries, to heal you. In fact, we as Catholics have "a moral obligation to use ordinary or proportionate means of preserving one's life…which in the judgment of the patient offers a reasonable hope of benefit, and does not entail excessive burden or impose excessive expense on the family or the community."[34]

Friends, the Catholic church isn't going to get into a play-by-play of what every line in your medical directives should or should not say, or what medical treatment is appropriate for every different person under every different scenario. That would be impossible for anyone to do, especially in advance of a complex medical event. Instead, the church sets

---

33   1 Corinthians 6:19

34   Ethical and Religious Directives for the Catholic Health Care Services, Sixth Edition, page 20-21.

forth biblical truths, ethical standards, and boundaries for human life to consider, knowing how personal and unique each individual situation can be. Catholic teachings ultimately leave the real-life judgment calls on medical decisions to the patient (or their advocate), to make plans and decisions according to God's will and their own personal conscience. Afterall, we are the ones who must stand before God and give him an accounting of our lives, including how we treated our human bodies.

God has made clear that when it comes to His will and His boundaries for human life, that "no man has authority over the day of his death".[35] Only God has the exclusive authority to bring us home to eternal life. Therefore, we cannot create medical directives or make medical decisions that will result in euthanasia (suicide), whether through an intentional act or an omission. While hopefully none of us are intentionally planning on ending our lives, you'd be surprised that many modern medical directives include provisions that may result in an act or omission that may cause euthanasia.

One of the most common acts or omissions that can cause euthanasia is when a patient has a medical directive that directs physicians to cease administering artificial nutrition and hydration if the patient is in a *persistent* vegetative state in which the patient can reasonably expect to live indefinitely with such assistance. The church believes artificial nutrition and hydration in those situations is a basic human

---

35   Ecclesiastes 8:8

right, just like bathing you and keeping you well-kept if you cannot do this yourself.

However, Catholic teachings acknowledge that there are limitations to life-sustaining procedures, including artificial nutrition and hydration, especially in cases where it "cannot reasonably be expected to prolong life or when it would be excessively burdensome for the patient, or would cause significant physical discomfort, for example, resulting from complications in the use of the means employed."[36] In those circumstances, the intended benefit of artificial nutrition administration may be overshadowed by the harm (i.e. fluid overload, congestion, pneumonitis, aspiration pneumonia) which likely will not prolong life but may add unneeded suffering to the dying person.

Furthermore, the church also understands that from a practical standpoint, that not everybody has access to advanced medical care, or the financial resources to pay for it, or that many of us are simply at the natural end of a terminal illness or our lifespan. Life-prolonging procedures in those circumstances might then be deemed extraordinary and impractical.

In the special case of artificial nutrition and hydration, we must further ask the question "will the withdrawal of nutrition and hydration allow the person to die, or kill the person? When it will allow a person to die from an underlying con-

---

36   Ethical and Religious Directives for the Catholic Health Care Services, Sixth Edition, page 20.

dition rather than unnecessarily prolonging their suffering, then it may be removed…However, when the withdrawal of nutrition and hydration is intended to kill the person, or will be the immediate and direct cause of doing so, quite apart from any disease or failure of their bodies, then to withdraw food and water would be an act of euthanasia, a grave sin against the natural law and the law of God."[37]

In the next two chapters, we will talk about the different types of medical directives you need to create to ensure all your medical decisions are made in compliance with Catholic moral teachings, with detailed instruction regarding your end-of-life care and your spiritual care. While we cannot anticipate every major medical event you may face, your medical directives must be clear and comprehensive enough so that medical professionals, hospital administrators, and the courts are fully aware of your wishes, and that they can be honored even if you are not lucid, or your medical agent is unavailable or unwilling to act. You should further instruct all persons involved with your medical care to consult with a priest or turn to the National Catholic Bioethics Center (ncbcenter.org) if further clarity or instructions are needed for a particular concern or decision.

In the end, after you've done all that you can to ensure your complete medical care, trust that the grace of our Lord Jesus Christ will be with you and all those assisting you.

---

37   Ethical and Religious Directives for the Catholic Health Care Services, Sixth Edition, page 20.

Chapter 16

WHAT YOUR MEDICAL DIRECTIVES SHOULD INCLUDE

Your medical directives should include your wishes for your complete medical care, which is sometimes formalized in one-single legal document or sometimes through multiple legal documents. The important thing is to make sure all the aspects that we cover below are included and that they are fully accessible by your loved ones and decision-makers during an emergency. You will also want to file a copy of your medical directives with your estate planning lawyer, your local hospital, and with your doctor's office.

Here are the different directives to include:

Living Will

Your medical directives will typically include a section, or a stand-alone document known as a living will, which expresses your wishes surrounding life-sustaining procedures if you are in a permanent vegetative state, or your death is imminent, or you have a terminal illness. The living will typically includes a statement that for your living will to be effective, your physicians must determine that there can be no recovery from your terminal or vegetative condition, and that your death is imminent. It typically forbids life-sustaining procedures in those situations, which often includes nutrition and hydration administered by invasive procedures; antibiotics; ventilators, pacemakers, renal dialysis, or any other mechanical devices designed to assist the functioning of organs; transfusion of blood and blood products; and cardiac or cardiopulmonary resuscitative procedures.

But many living wills go even further and forbid these life-prolonging procedures if you "can no longer experience a meaningful life" or "are in a persistent vegetative state", meaning your condition is ongoing but your death may not be necessarily imminent. As we discussed earlier, mandating the removal of life support under those circumstances is too broad, and could result in euthanasia. Instead, if you choose to express your general wishes surrounding life-sustaining procedures through a living will, you must ensure that the living will works in conjunction with your medial power of attorney (which we will talk about next), so that your agent (and not others who may not share your beliefs) can ultimately make these unpredictable life and death calls in real time, and in harmony with Catholic moral teachings. Beware of pre-checking boxes on a living will without proper guidance, and without having other necessary safeguards that ensure your complete medical care and prevent euthanasia.

Pregnancy Override Clause for Living Wills

There has been a lot of attention in the media lately over women who have fallen into a vegetative state while pregnant. Through modern medicine and technology, doctors may be able to save an unborn child even when the mother becomes incapacitated. It may be a situation you or your spouse have never contemplated, but it's one that women in their child-bearing years should address in their medical directives.

If this potential situation applies to you, would you want to be kept alive artificially in a permanent vegetative state if you were pregnant? If so, you will want to include a "pregnancy override clause" in your living will that states you would not want to be removed from life support if you are pregnant and if the doctors determine the baby can develop properly and be safely delivered.

When you consider this difficult issue, you need to work with an attorney who understands all possible legal and moral ramifications of your decision, such as:

- What laws, if any, does your state have regarding pregnancy and incapacity?
- What if you were early in your pregnancy?

- What if the doctors determined your unborn child was not developing properly because of the event that caused your irreversible vegetative condition?

- Would you want your spouse to ultimately make the call, or would you want your family to have to abide by your pre-set wishes?

- What do your moral beliefs and conscience dictate when pregnancy and incapacity collide?

It's interesting because when discussing this possible scenario with different priests, there does not seem to be a bright line consensus on what's morally required in such a situation. Is there a moral duty for a pregnant woman to be kept alive on machines to continue growing an unborn child? Is this considered ordinary or extra-ordinary means? Is it a case-by-case decision to be made in real time? Like the approach for applying or withholding life-sustaining procedures, you may wish for your pregnancy override clause to express your desired outcome, conditional on your Catholic beliefs, as applied by your trusted medical decision maker to your unique situation in real time.

Advanced Health Care Directive

An **Advanced Health Care Directive** (also known as a Health Care Power of Attorney) works in conjunction with your living will and allows you to designate someone to make and carry out your medical decisions for you if you lack capacity to make these decisions yourself. It provides instructions on your medical evaluation and treatment, long-term care and hospice, your wishes for staying in your residence versus a facility, who can hire and fire your doctors, and your wishes when it comes to pain relief, psychiatric treatment, organ donation, and other important decisions that must be made for your care.

It's imperative when selecting the person you trust to make these decisions, that you choose someone who shares or will honor your values and beliefs system, meaning, they will strive to make decisions for you that you would make for yourself. As we talked about earlier when discussing living wills, there are so many variables when it comes to accepting or rejecting life-prolonging procedures, and someone often must make these game time decisions for us based on science and faith, within God's boundaries for human life. Make sure when selecting this person you trust to make these decisions if you cannot, that you take time to really talk with them, including how you wish for those decisions to be made, who else you wish for them to consult with if there's medical or moral uncertainty, and most importantly, your desire that such decisions are made in line with God's laws and Catholic teachings.

Furthermore, this trustworthy person must also be willing to stand up to family pressure stemming from others' personal views, fears, sorrow, or guilt, and to carry out your wishes regardless. You will also want to name back-up agents who can step in if for some reason your trustworthy person is unavailable to perform these duties.

Organ Donation

Choosing to become an organ donor is choosing to give life to another person in your death. Catholic teachings encourage, but do not require, people to donate their organs and bodily tissue for ethically legitimate purposes for transplant or medical research.

However, before organ donation occurs, it's imperative that all morally obligatory and appropriate means were used to preserve one's life as previously discussed, and that the potential for organ donation was not a factor in one's end-of-life care. Because the protocols for organ donation continue to evolve and the standards and guidelines in your state may not necessarily reflect Catholic moral teachings, your medical agent should consult with your priest or the National Catholic Bioethics Center for further instruction and clarification if there is any uncertainty regarding the procurement or proper use of your organ donation.

If you would like to pre-authorize organ donation, it's best to do so by including a clause in your medical directives that authorizes your medical agent to make such gifts on your behalf provided organs are procured and used in compliance with Catholic moral teachings.

HIPAA Authorization

Your medical directives should also include a section, or stand-alone form, that authorizes certain people you trust to receive your private medical information. Without this legal authorization, your private medical information cannot be shared with others. This is because Congress passed a law known as the Health Insurance Portability and Accountability Act (HIPAA) that limits the use, disclosure, or release of your health information without your consent.

I have a colleague who shared with me that her son threw a pool party at their home when he was in college and suffered a major brain injury from a diving board accident. When friends contacted her and her husband, they rushed to the hospital, only to be told by staff that they could not share his status or any medical information with them because of HIPAA. You can imagine the heartbreak and frustration too many families experience from this very common situation when a loved one is seriously hurt but they don't have legal directives authorizing disclosure of their medical information. That's why it's imperative to have legal directives that list authorized persons who can receive your medical information.

Many people who execute a HIPAA authorization make it contingent on them becoming incapacitated; meaning, these people can't access your medical information until a physician has officially certified your incapacity. This can cause significant delays, which would likely prevent your authorized persons from getting information right away when they arrive at the hospital. For these reasons, many people choose to make their HIPAA authorization effective immediately, and not contingent on incapacity. You will want to be careful that you are only authorizing people you trust, who will not inappropriately access your medical records outside of a serious medical event.

Chapter 17
YOUR SPIRITUAL CARE DURING a LIFE-THREATENING SITUATION

Jesus understands first-hand how physical suffering, or the prospect of death, can cause us (and our loved ones) anxiety, grief, anger, sadness and even a crisis of faith. He himself personally experienced the human reality of suffering when he pleaded to the Father in the Garden of Gethsemane before going to the cross. "My Father, if it is possible, let this cup pass from me; yet, not as I will, but as you will."[38]

While we read of numerous accounts in the Holy Bible where Christ "took on our infirmities and bore our diseases," Jesus did not heal everyone who was sick. While even in today's times "the holy spirit gives to some a special charism of healing so as to make manifest the power of the grace of

---

38   Matthew 26:39

the risen Lord, even the most intense prayers do not always obtain the healing of an illness."[39] Instead, "Christ's healings were signs of the coming of the kingdom of God. They announced a more radical healing; the victory over sin and death through his Passover."[40]

How can we receive the spiritual care we need to sustain us if our physical bodies are suffering? While the concern of others, the meals that are sent, and the excellent medical care we receive all provide us much needed comfort and care, it is ultimately the power of prayer that can help us endure our suffering.

Prayer is one of the most beautiful gifts we have as human beings. Prayer is a direct line of communication between us and our Father who loves us and created us. It's a free call, anytime, anyplace, available for anyone, and it always goes through. While it's not always answered in a way that our human minds can accept or comprehend, it is always received with love, understanding, compassion, and care, and with the promise that even if our body is not physically healed, God will always heal our soul.

If you really think about that promise for a moment, it's quite liberating. There are many of us whose bodies have been harmed, or are ill, or are disabled, or aging, but Catholic teachings proclaim that the soul that is housed inside a

---

39   Catechism 1508

40   Catechism 1505

suffering body can always be fully healed through the love and grace of Jesus Christ.

I visited last year with a friend during the thick of battling an aggressive form of cancer. While still beautiful on the outside, her body visibly showed the damage from the cancer and chemo treatments. Just as one complication from the cancer was resolved, another one seemed to pop up. She had to step away from her successful law practice and rely on family just to get dressed at times or eat a meal. At that time, there were no definitive assurances that she would be physically healed.

Yet, despite all of this, I had never seen someone more at peace.

"This cancer has been awful," she shared. "It's literally destroyed my bones. But I have never felt so close to God and to my family. Even the power struggles I had with my mother-in-law are gone. She has done so much for me and my girls and has been there for me every step of the way. I am just so grateful to be alive. I feel free. I don't care anymore about making money, or having my law firm, or holding on to trauma from my past. I just want to be with my husband and daughters and enjoy the rest of my life."

That, my friends, is a prime example of someone whose body was physically suffering, but whose soul had been undeniably healed. Thanks be to God.

Jesus has promised each and every one of us that He can do for us what He has done for my friend and countless others. When we come to Him in prayer and recognize the small blessings and mercies we receive each and every day, He will carry us through and heal our souls. This is why we should continually pray for a special strength and grace that only He can provide during our greatest times of need.

The Catholic Church recognizes the power that prayer can have on the suffering person. We have a very special prayer that is offered to the sick through the sacrament called the Anointing of the Sick that is designed and reserved for those facing a life-threatening disease or condition, which is available to the suffering person as often as they feel it is helpful. In St. James we are told, "Is anyone among you sick? He should summon the presbyters of the church, and they should pray over him and anoint [him] with oil in the name of the Lord, and the prayer of faith will save the sick person, and the Lord will raise him up. If he has committed any sins, he will be forgiven."[41]

While the Anointing of the Sick does not always heal the physical body, it provides special graces to those who are sick and suffering so the soul can be healed. First, this special prayer and sacrament asks God to send the Holy Spirit to help comfort and strengthen the suffering person. This allows the suffering person to have the special grace and courage needed to endure their challenges. Second, it helps the suffering person unite himself with Christ's Passion and uniquely participate in the saving work of Jesus. For those who are truly suffering, the concept of Christ suffering on the cross

---

41   James 5: 13-14

takes on a whole new personal meaning and comprehension. Third, the suffering person through uniting with the passion and death of Christ can then contribute to the good of the People of God and help sanctify the church. Often, one's suffering can bring out the best in the community as people rise to the occasion to pray and care for the suffering person. And fourth, the Anointing of the Sick helps the suffering person prepare for their final journey to eternal life.[42]

I have a client now who is battling stage four cancer and has been given only a few years to live with the current treatments available. He does not consider himself religious although he was raised as a Catholic. During our most recent conversation, he asked me to add his name to the prayer list at my parish. He said, "Laura, I have four different church congregations praying for me right now and I would love if yours could add me to the list. I believe in the power of prayer. It's strange how this experience is bringing me so much love and amazing people into my life to be with me on this journey. It really is so…wonderful, as crazy as that may sound."

Prayer changes everything. It's that simple. It's that profound.

At the end of one's life, we are also invited to receive another special sacrament—Viaticum— where we can receive the Eucharist one last time before passing over to the Father. Receiving the Eucharist in that final moment is "particularly significant and important as it is the seed of

---

42   Catechism 1520-1523

eternal life and the power of the resurrection, according to the words of the Lord."[43] Jesus promises us that "whoever eats my flesh and drinks my blood has eternal life, and I will raise him on the last day."[44] What a beautiful promise for any of us who are sick or suffering, or have lost someone we love, to know with confidence that none of us will ever truly die, but instead live forever.

Need medical directives that ensure your **complete physical & spiritual care?**

SCAN the QR code for access.

I am reminded again of my son's physician who spoke about how many suffering people have no one here on earth to love them or even drive them home from a surgery. Yet through these two beautiful sacraments—the Anointing of the Sick and Viaticum—and through God's everyday love for us, we can rest assured that we will never truly be alone in our suffering. God is always with us, loving us, comforting us, healing our bodies, and always healing our souls. None of us should go through a major medical crisis without the

---

43   Catechism 1524

44   John 6:54

spiritual care that He longs to give us during our greatest times of need.

Be sure that your medical directives specifically express your wishes for your spiritual care. Include your wishes that you receive regular pastoral care, the Anointing of the Sick, Reconciliation, and Viaticum. By doing this, you are pre-inviting Jesus to be with you every step of your journey and provide you with a supernatural care that only He can provide.

Chapter 18
YOUR FINAL GOODBYE

In an ideal world, you will live a very long and happy life and have the chance to say goodbye to everyone you love and express what's in your heart before you leave this earth. But in the real world, that's not how it typically happens. Not one single person is guaranteed another tomorrow, and too many people leave this world with many things unsaid which can leave a hole in the hearts of the loved ones left behind. "I never got the chance to say goodbye." I have heard those words too many times from grieving clients who lost a loved one all too soon. How many people do you know who have saved voicemails from someone they loved and lost, just to hear their voice one more time?

That's why I want to encourage you to take the time now, while you are still healthy and able, to capture what's in your heart for your loved ones in case you don't get the opportunity to say it later. This is typically accomplished through what we call a Legacy Interview, where you can audio or video record your special memories, words of wisdom, and best wishes for those left behind.

My law firm helped a husband and wife who were trying to be proactive and set up an estate plan just in case anything unexpected should happen. As part of that routine process, we had them record a Legacy Interview through which they could record their special memories, words of wisdom, and anything they'd like to say to their loved ones. The husband had no idea at the time that he would soon be diagnosed with stage four brain cancer, and would die within months, leaving his wife and three young children behind.

When I learned of his diagnosis, I personally double-checked their Legacy Interview just to confirm it was perfectly recorded. I happened to click on a part of the interview where he was describing each of his three young children in detail—from what he liked about them, what he saw in them, and how much he loved them. And then he said something I will never forget: "the one thing I can tell already about my kids, even though they are young, is that they are strong kids, and I know that no matter what comes against them in life, that they will overcome."

What other opportunity would these young children left behind ever have to hear their own father's voice, in his own words, describing what he saw in them, and hearing the confidence he had in them and their strength, had he not taken the time to record what was in his heart while he was still living and able? You can imagine what a priceless gift this was for his grieving family members, and how much his children will cherish this recording as they grow older and continue to navigate his loss.

What's in your heart today that you would want to share, one more time, with the people you love most? All your love and dreams for your family shouldn't be lost when you die. As you go to record your own Legacy Interview and express what's in your heart, experts tell us to be sure to include these five expressions so you can die in peace, and your loved ones can live in peace:

1. **I love you**. It seems straight forward but these are the three most powerful words most people long to hear from those we love. Even in cultures where these words are not regularly expressed, I can assure you your loved ones want to hear this.

2. **Thank you**. It's important to express our gratitude for the joy and devotion others brought to our lives, and for all the good times we had here.

3. **I'm sorry**. Who longs to hear those words from you? None of us are perfect, and it's okay to admit where we wish we had done better.

4. **I forgive you**. Those grudges in our heart formed for a reason, but when a heart is truly one with the Lord, we have to let them go. We are called to live in peace.

5. **Forgive me**. It's not easy to ask others for forgiveness, but it will bring both you and your loved ones great peace by asking for forgiveness for our mistakes and failures.

And on that note, let's not wait until we are gone for others to hear these five expressions. God longs to heal our broken relationships, right past wrongs, drive anger from our hearts, and calls us to live in peace with one another. I hope we all have the courage and humility, myself included, to express these words today. You deserve to live each day of your life feeling happy and whole.

Once you record your Legacy Interview, keep it in a safe place and let your loved ones and your estate planning lawyer know it exists and where to locate it. I promise you this will be a cherished gift to your family that will not only comfort them, but also bless the generations to come. You are special to your loved ones so do not forget to preserve yourself when planning for everyone you love!

Ready to record your personal legacy interview?

SCAN the QR code for the top ten prompts you'll want to discuss!

Chapter 19
YOUR FINAL SEND-OFF

When you are called home to eternal life, your loved ones will likely want to celebrate your life and remember the wonderful, loving, person that you are. They will want to honor you and gather to give you a proper send-off. They will also want to receive comfort from all those left behind here. They say the funeral or celebration of life is meant to get you to where you need to go, and the living to where they need to go.

It goes without saying that a loved one's death typically causes those left behind profound grief, sorrow, loss, and pain, even if we know our loved one lived a full and happy life. I continually hear from clients whose parents lived their full, natural lifespan, "I know it was her time, but I still lost my mom, and it hurts." And for those who lost a loved one prematurely, you can imagine the pain even with great faith. That's why our wishes for our final send-off should not only consider our wishes, but also what's comforting for those left behind.

In the Catholic tradition, we typically have a Catholic funeral for our final send-off when we leave this earth. However, a Catholic funeral is not a sacrament, and therefore not mandatory. The church understands that the living of the deceased may not share the same faith, or that a Catholic funeral may not be feasible due to local customs or circumstances. What's best for you and your loved ones is a decision you should make.

Catholics usually have multiple ceremonies in honor of the deceased. First, there is a vigil service, which is also called a wake or a rosary service, where family and friends gather to pray the rosary and share special memories. Next, there is a funeral Mass, followed by the graveside committal.

A Catholic funeral typically is comprised of four key components, regardless of whether it is held in a home, a church, or a cemetery: (1) A greeting of faith that reminds us to have hope because Christ has overcome death, (2) The liturgy that conveys the Christian perspective of death in light of the risen Christ, (3) The Eucharist (provided the funeral takes place in church) which invites the surviving family members to live in communion with their departed loved one by receiving the Eucharist and through prayer; and (4) A final goodbye to you and asking God to receive you in His care. "We shall never be separated (from our departed loved one), for we live for Christ and now we are united with Christ as we go toward him…we shall all be together in Christ."[45]

---

45   Catechism 1684-2688

As Catholics, we believe that while death may separate our body and soul, that both will be reunited on the last day when Christ raises us from the dead. For this reason, the Catholic Church prefers, but does not require, that the faithful be buried.[46] "By burying the bodies of the faithful, the Church confirms her faith in the resurrection of the body."[47] Furthermore, "burial in a cemetery or another sacred place adequately corresponds to the piety and respect owed to the bodies of the faithful departed who through baptism have become temples of the Holy Spirit…"[48]

The church recognizes however that due to "sanitary, economic or social considerations," that some may opt for cremation, which is permissible if it does not violate the wishes of the departed or is chosen for reasons contrary to Christian doctrine. Ashes "must be laid to rest in a sacred place such as a cemetery of dedicated area in a church." Only in grave and exceptional cases dependent on cultural conditions of a localized nature may ashes be kept in a domestic residence. Even then, it must be approved by the Church.[49]

At the date of this publication, the church recently published that it is possible for the ashes of baptized persons to be

---

46   Instruction regarding the burial of the deceased and the conservation of the ashes in the case of cremation, 2016.

47   Instruction regarding the burial of the deceased and the conservation of the ashes in the case of cremation, 2016.

48   Instruction regarding the burial of the deceased and the conservation of the ashes in the case of cremation, 2016.

49   Dicasterium Pro Doctrina Fidei, Reply to His Eminence Cardinal Matteo Maria Zuppi, Archbishop of Bologna, December 9, 2023

commingled and set aside in a defined and permanent sacred place so long as the identity of each person is preserved so as not to lose memory of their names, and that the ecclesiastical authority, in compliance with civil norms, may consider and evaluate a request by a family member to preserve in an appropriate way a minimal part of the relative's ashes in a place of significance for the history of the deceased person, provided that every type pantheistic, naturalistic, or nihilistic misunderstanding is ruled out and also provided that the ashes of the deceased are kept in a sacred place. It's unclear if the church's statement was a broad shift in policy or is limited to special cases arising out of necessity.[50]

One of the comments we often get asked as Catholics is why do you have so many rules and restrictions on what you can do with your own body, even down to what you can do with your remains?! I understand that and sometimes ask questions like this myself. But, what I've come to understand in all my research for this book and in working with those facing death, is that our Catholic teachings surrounding our human bodies aren't restrictions—they are *protections*. God wants our bodies treated respectfully and with care, under all circumstances, by all persons, including our own selves. In fact, our human bodies are so special to God that He has literally promised to raise them on the last day—not just our souls, but also our bodies.

---

50   Dicasterium Pro Doctrina Fidei, Reply to His Eminence Cardinal Matteo Maria Zuppi, Archbishop of Bologna, December 9, 2023

As you formalize your wishes for your final send-off, be sure to include your wishes and reasoning for the type of services you want, and for the disposition of your remains. You may also wish to go further and specify things like who you wish to speak or eulogize you at your wake or funeral, who you want as pallbearers, what songs you want to be sung, where you want to be laid to rest, etc. Even making a notation that you do not have a strong preference on things like that can be incredibly helpful as surviving family members often have their own strong personal feelings and opinions on what they feel is best. We can trust that if we bring these decisions to God through prayer that He will help us know what is best for our unique situations.

Chapter 20

YOUR LEGACY

As Catholics, we believe that all people are created for eternal life. We also believe that the love we have for others, and the good we have done in the world, can continue to be a light in this world long after we are gone. That time you took to teach a child the difference between right and wrong will continue to guide them even when you are gone. That smile you gave your spouse every morning will be engrained as an image in their mind and soul and light up their day even after you are gone. The money you donated for our brothers and sisters in need for meals, clothing, medicine, and care, will make a difference long after you are gone. Your life has made a difference to your loved ones, and to the world, for the better.

But for far too many people, their legacy becomes lost or overshadowed when they fail to properly plan. To recap, right now, without you having created your own estate plan for your end of life wishes, you are subject to the plan your state government created for you:

- Your children may be placed in temporary foster care and a judge will have to choose a guardian through a long and painful court process that can put family members against one another.

- Your loved ones may have to spend 2-3 years embroiled in probate court proceedings that causes unnecessary delays and an interruption of financial support, which can cost tens of thousands of dollars if not more.

- The money you left behind for your family's care can be taken by creditors, predators, lawsuits, future divorces, and ill-intentioned third parties.

- Your money can only go to your next of kin and cannot be used to support any of your other moral obligations to others or help ensure the universal destination of goods.

- Your money can end up going toward unnecessary taxes that could have been avoided or mitigated through proper planning.

- Your medical decisions might not be made by who you wanted or the way you wanted, and might even result in violating God's laws for your proper care and treatment.

- You might not receive the spiritual care that God longs to provide you during a medical crisis.

- You may not get the chance to say goodbye to your loved ones and provide them with the peace they need to move forward and be happy.

I know this is not the right course of action for your family. But unless you act now while you are living and able, your loved ones will become part of the staggering 70% statistic of families who end up in court when a loved one becomes incapacitated or dies. Please don't let this happen to your family.

You have the power to change everything.

You can create an estate plan that ensures complete protection for you and your loved ones.

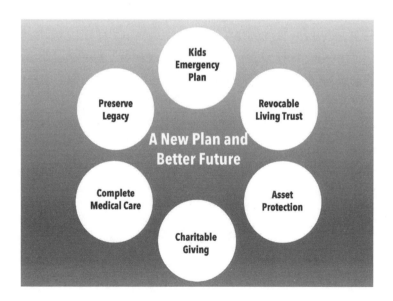

This is the outcome that your family deserves—children raised in love and the faith by the people you've chosen, money immediately accessible to loved ones that can't be stripped away by ill-intentioned third parties or tied up in court, your time, talents, and treasures being used to bless the lives of your family and community, your medical decisions being made that ensures your complete care, and a legacy that goes on for generations to come. Today is always the best day to plan for the people we love. I know you can do it!

As we close out our time together, I want to thank you personally for all the good you are doing in the world each and every day. Thank you for being part of God's work here on earth and being a light in the world. We are all in this life together so let's be kind to each other, especially to those who believe or live differently from you or me. Let others see the face of God through the love you give and through your charitable giving. I pray that God will bless you with a spirit of abundance, keep you and your loved ones safe, and hold you in the palm of His hand.

ACKNOWLEDGEMENTS

I am incredibly thankful to God for blessing me with the incredible opportunity to write "Guided by Grace" and for opening doors I never thought possible. The spirit of kindness and collaboration I witnessed in this project from everyone involved has been truly heartwarming.

Thank you to my husband, Joshua Meier, Esq., and our children, Conrad, Jack, Kate, and Andrew for the time and support needed to write a book that personally means so much to me.

My deepest gratitude goes to Most Reverend Kevin William Vann, J.C.D., D.D., for granting "Guided by Grace" the imprimatur, and to Reverend William B. Goldin, S.Th.D., for the nihil obstat. I'm also profoundly grateful to Colin Donovan, STL, Vice President of Theology at EWTN, for his willingness to review and endorse the book, offering invaluable time and guidance throughout.

I must express my sincere appreciation to Very Rev. David Andel, J.C.L., Dr. Vincent Nguyen, Dr. Suzanne Strom, Keith Page, and all those who contributed their ideas and content, enriching this work beyond measure. Your wisdom and support were essential to its completion.

Acknowledging the angels in my life, Cathy Collins (who deserves a halo), Jim Normandin, Anthony Vultaggio, Steve Cameron, Kathleen Hurtt, Shannon Eusey, my pastor Father Steve Sallot, and my father-in-law David Meier, for their guidance and support. My publishing team, Tom Costello, Francine Costello, and Jason Price at Word Association Publishers, have been nothing short of amazing, offering kindness, patience, and hard work.

Finally, I am thankful to Dr. Timothy You for showing our family what it means to have the complete care that Jesus longs for all of us to have during our greatest times of need.

ABOUT THE AUTHOR

Laura Meier, Esq. is a California family trust lawyer, best-selling author, and television news personality. She has spoken at Fortune 500 companies, and her work has been regularly featured by national media outlets including NBC, ABC, CBS, FOX, Forbes, and more. She and her husband, Joshua Meier, Esq., own the Meier Law Firm in Newport Beach, California, serving families with their estate planning needs throughout the state. The Meiers are the proud parents of four great kids and are parishioners of Our Lady Queen of Angels Catholic Church. You can contact Laura for speaking engagements or your family's estate planning needs by emailing her at office@meierfirm.com.

BONUS QR CODES:

Do you need to work with a lawyer?

What should this type of planning cost?

Where can I make a difference with
my time, talents, and gifts?

LAURA K. MEIER, ESQ.

450 Newport Center Drive, Suite 500
Newport Beach, California 92660

www.guidedbygraceplanning.com

WA

ENDORSEMENTS FOR GUIDED BY GRACE

imprimatur **granted February 8, 2024**
by Most Reverend Kevin William Vann, J.C.D.,D.D.

nihil obstat **granted December 28, 2023**
by Reverend William B. Goldin, S.Th.D.

"Each of us will reach the end of our life at a time we cannot know (Mt. 25:13). Our spiritual readiness is paramount, as Our lord reminds us, but our material preparation is also important. Laura Meier has written an eminently useful book, packed with practical advice for end-of-life planning, and imbued with the wisdom of the Church! It will do incalculable good!"

Colin B. Donovan, STL,
V.P. of Theology, EWTN

"Ensuring the future care of our families is a fundamental of Christian stewardship. The work of Laura Meier, particularly this book, offers a wonderful example of how families can embrace this biblical imperative."

Michael Murphy, Executive Director
International Catholic Stewardship Council

"I highly recommend Guided by Grace by attorney Laura Meier. She writes from personal experience, and possesses the talent to comprehend the gravity of those critical, life-impacting moments in our lives. Moreover, she has the natural ability to communicate these critical concepts to the audience, and emphasize the importance of planning. The book is packed with pearls to be able to handle the sometimes complex legalities of taking care of our family members through life's challenges. Congratulations to an accomplished writer! Thank you for sharing your difficult story, and letting me be a part of your "Catholic Journey.""

Timothy T. You MD

"A unique book that weaves together the Catholic faith and the importance of making sure you and your loved ones are cared for throughout their whole life. The book highlights Catholic teachings from the Holy Bible and reinforces through several practical examples why it is important to have an effective trust, advanced healthcare directives, and other key components to insure your wishes and your beliefs are upheld. As a long-term healthcare executive, I have seen too many times where families, patients, friends, and those involved are torn, confused, and frustrated without having the appropriate legal plan in place ahead of time. This book gives you the simple steps to follow, real world examples, and the confidence of the Holy Bible and your faith to design the best way to protect yourself and your loved ones. It is very refreshing to have a book with such helpful legal advice and an author that also believes in the power of prayer and God's sovereignty."

Jeremy Zoch, PhD.,
Former CEO at Providence St. Joseph
Hospital of Orange

"Laura Meier has created a groundbreaking way of incorporating Catholic beliefs and values with estate planning. Guided by Grace covers all areas of estate planning including how to proactively and properly plan to care for children, protecting ourselves with medical directives, and avoiding probate by establishing a living trust. All along the way it incorporates passages from the Catechism of the Catholic church, bible verses, and Catholic values to show the importance of estate planning and to guide us as we create our own estate plan. The author's personal stories are relatable and create feelings of positivity and hope. A must read for all Catholics to help us as we navigate issues we face in our daily lives and discern the legacy we leave for family and the greater good."

Shannon Eusey,
CEO Beacon Pointe Advisors